H

O

The River of

P

E

Translation by Eun-Joo Ryo

Cover design and graphics work by Imago Studios
458 Hermitage Dr., Deerfield, IL 60015
imagodesign@hotmail.com

autobiography

by

Sun-Tae Kim

Contents

Book I
The Adventure of My Life

Book II
Spiritual Discipline from the School of the Wilderness

Book III
Mission Field Episodes

BOOK IV
Unforgettable Stories and Other Thoughts

Epilogue

The Sun-Tae Kim I Know

Forward

An Exemplary Christian
of This Generation

In I Corinthians 11:1, the Apostle Paul encourages us by saying "Follow my example as I follow the example of Christ."

The presence of many exemplary figures in different sectors of the community establishes a healthy and orderly society. This principle also applies to families. Children take after their parents. If parents show constant affection towards their kids as they diligently and joyfully served their neighbors, the children will also grow up with such characteristics. Such families might face financial difficulties and other forms of hardship but because they do not lack love and affection, they will remain solid.

There aren't too many role models worthy of emulation in our society today. One by one such exemplary figures have left only to be replaced by corrupted individuals who pollute our entire society, slowly poisoning it, which will ultimately lead to its destruction. It is truly a tragic reality.

More than any other time in history, we long for exemplary leaders. And for me to have met Reverend Kim at such a point in time as this is a great privilege and joy. It is unnecessary for me to go into details about how he has triumphed with his faith, living a life worthy of emulation as he overcame all obstacles and hardships for the sake of giving hope to the blind since all that is already too well known. Up to this day, he lives to give new life, strong faith and hope to the visually disabled through eye operations. His missionary work to the blind is not limited only to Korea. He has already visited many other countries including China, restoring sight to the blind.

Reverend Kim is truly a remarkable servant of love who puts his faith to work. Such qualities make him a great Christian who is worthy of emulation. On June first of 1998, in recognition of all the work he had accomplished and will accomplish in the future, he was honored with the Ho-Ahm Social Service Award. In addition to this, his work has been recognized and approved by the government and leaders of every social class.

It is moving indeed to finally read Reverend Kim's published version of his autobiography as he tells his story from the inside out. It is my heart-felt desire that this book will be widely read so that he will be recognized as a person to be imitated, and that many people will indeed become more like him through this book.

Yoon-Bae Uh

President of Soongsil University

Preface

The Paradoxical Love From Heaven

My life, from the worldly point of view, is a life of accumulated resentments. But had I not a chance to throw off my resentments, I could have never become friends with those who had as many resentments as I did, let alone relieving them. I cannot deny that I would have become devoted to the cause of opening people's eyes if I did not endure through my resentful childhood experiences.

There is hardly any difference between my story and the story of the female protagonist in Chung Joon Lee's fiction, *Suh-Pyun-Jae* (Tragic Korean Opera). There is a part where the father intentionally makes his daughter blind by secretly drugging her so that she can be a better traditional Korean opera singer. Since the daughter knew that becoming blind was a way to accumulate resentment to sing better tragic operas, she did not let her father know that she knew what he had done to her. As a result, the daughter was able to become the greatest opera singer of her time. The story goes to show that true artistic ability can only become manifest through the paradoxical process of accumulating resentment and relieving it.

How are we to interpret the paradoxical love of the father who blinds his own daughter for the sake of her singing career? My life also, cannot be explained apart from the paradoxical love from above. The reason lies in fact that I have found my calling in my own loss of sight.

I was not born blind. When I was ten years old, I lost my sight during the Korean War. I had to live in despair having lost my world. However, I was able to overcome abuses and humiliation because I discovered the wisdom of letting go off my resentments. I can only thank God for giving me the strength to carry my cross victoriously. Whenever I faced countless failures and difficulties during the Korean War, I prayed to God, "If you will only save me from this situation, I will devote my life to You as a pastor."

The reason I could become friends with the visually disabled is because I too have drank from the bitter cup of blindness. I started writing this book to give much needed hope to a frightened young generation and the visually disabled by showing them how I have triumphed over my obstacles and trials.

I cannot forget the devotion and encouragement given by many of my faithful friends, teachers, sponsors and co-workers in the missionary work for the visually disabled. The burning sense of calling to work for the blind constantly moves me to action. The secret lies in the existence of my personal Saviour, Jesus Christ, my object of love and faith.

I have my quiet time at 3:40 in the morning. I plan out the best possible way to use my day most efficiently and effectively. Only after doing so, I head out to my office. Since a visually disabled person must move more shrewdly than others, I go and come back from work when I know there will be least volume of traffic in the morning and evening. Since Korean society still lags behind other developed countries in its consideration for the visually disabled, overcoming such obstacles poses as a big problem.

The Siloam Eye Hospital is a place where the blind receives sight. The construction of the building started in December of 1981, and I have been actively ministering to restore sight to the blind through eyesight recovery operations since February of 1986. The convicting question, "Who is your neighbor?" posed by Jesus made me into a friend for the blind.

I give glory to God for the opportunity to publish my very own autobiography. I would like to share the joy of this publication with the friends and churches all over the world who helped our Siloam ministry with their prayers and financial contributions. I would also like to express thanks to all the Siloam employees who worked so hard in making this publication possible. I sincerely wish that this book may be the source through which the 200,000 blind and 5 million visually challenged in Korea will regain their sight.

I give all the glory to God who has and will use my life as his pleasing instrument of love, and who has given me unimaginable joy and happiness.

Sun-Tae Kim
Siloam Eye Hospital

B
O
O
K

I

The Adventure of My Life

Into the World of Darkness

The Remains of the Korean War

To borrow the expression of the Apostle Paul, the scars I carry are reminders of the cross of Jesus Christ. In my case, the scars were inflicted on me by the Korean War. Although these scars of pain are thorns in my flesh, I now realize these are evidence of the miracle that has enabled me to work for His kingdom and His righteousness. Our national tragedy, the Korean War, not only left me an orphan but also, as the result of a bomb explosion, destroyed my sight. Despite everything, I believe these scars of the Korean War built up in me the character necessary to resolve sufferings and to stand strong.

Had I been pampered in a comfortable home as an only son, I would have led a most selfish life. How could I have become a friend of the blind and journey the sacrificial life of a pastor? Because the basic desire of man is to lead a comfortable and successful life, I would have lived out my life according to my basic instincts. However, the countless scars of suffering and pain have made me what I am today, a missionary called to work for the blind.

When I reflect about my loving Saviour ingraining my body with the marks of suffering, it reminds me of the accumulated resentment in my heart. Graciously, He transformed me into a healer of souls by allowing me to resolve the resentments of others as He gradually resolved mine. How could my finite mind fathom all the profound things He had planned for my life in His absolute sovereignty?

One thing I am sure of, is that without passing through the forests of hardship, suffering, rejection and despair, I would have never given birth to a great life. Thomas A. Kempis wrote, "As fire sharpens iron, suffering sharpens a righteous man." The scars inflicted upon me are upon my flesh. The scars I received from people who accused, oppressed, and abused me, are my medals as well as my scars of glory. If I had never resolved the pain I received through poverty, discrimination, and many abuses, my heart would have languished in hatred toward the world throughout my life. Not only would hatred have consumed me, but I would have also deteriorated mentally, living the life of a bitterly wounded animal by abusing myself and inflicting violence on others.

In the healing process from the many wounds I received, I am thankful to my Lord that He used all the resentments and complaints that resulted from my pain as an opportunity for creating new things. Imagine yourself in an extreme situation. It would be incredibly difficult to deal with the wrath and feelings of mortification without expressing them. But if you endure the pain, there is an altogether wonderful feeling that springs from the depths of your soul as that ball of resentment melts away. Such feelings always lead me to new beginnings as the hunger for life blazed anew within me. This is a profound mystery of life.

The Lost World

September 1941, I was born as the precious only son of the Kim family from Kyung-Ju during the fall harvest season. For a young boy who grew up without any hardships, a much unexpected tragedy was waiting.

It was June 25, 1950, and I was almost ten. The war, which would soon take away everything from my life, had erupted. When the North Korean People's Republic Army invaded the South, Seoul was destroyed in the blink of an eye. I can still clearly remember every frightening scene that took place that year.

As I recall, it was ten days after the war broke out. That last day I ate breakfast with my parents was a tragic day. The lives of my parents, as well as all our possessions, were later destroyed as a result of bombing. My life completely changed in just matter of seconds.

"Sun-Tae, let's eat breakfast." Even now, I can almost hear the gentle voice of my mother. I think my father, who was usually quiet, was worried that morning because he said to me during breakfast, "Sun Tae, the air raids are worsening. Be careful. Since this is war time, don't go too far, and never play dangerous pranks."

"Yes, Father," I replied.

After breakfast, I was busy playing with my friends. How was I to know that leaving my house in Shindang-Dong that morning would be the last time I would see my parents? What would I give if only I could reverse the events of that fateful day?

While playing, I got hungry and ran back to my house, but the house was gone. Then my eyes went blank, and I let out a loud cry. Fear gripped me. "Mom! Dad!" I went around the whole village screaming until my voice gave out, but I could not find a trace of them.

I became an orphan overnight. Being the only son without many relatives, I didn't know what to do. My next door neighbor's house was also destroyed in the bombing. Seoul became a sea of fire. It was a difficult situation for a little boy to handle.

I was starving without means of survival. To satisfy my stomach I had no choice but to beg. I walked from Shindang-Dong all the way to Wong Shim Ri, going door to door begging, "Please give me some food." Surprisingly, I was able to get food, but eating food given to me out of pity made me feel sad and sorry for myself. At night, I didn't know where to sleep. I spent that first hot summer night on the porch of someone's house as the mosquitoes feasted on me.

During August, I spent my days as a beggar. One day my eight friends and I went toward the Ddook Island to steal some watermelons.

"Hey, let's go out to Ddook Island for some good watermelon!"

"Sure. But what if we get caught?"

"There won't be any owner there during war time. Finder's keepers. Don't worry and follow us."

"Okay."

We were busy gulping down watermelons when a few of my friends were examining something they had found a little distance away. Suddenly I heard a loud explosion, and then I lost consciousness. I don't know how many hours passed.

"Oh my, you are so lucky. All your friends died when the bomb exploded but you survived. Heaven helped you."

But what was this? The blue sky, green pastures, flowing river, friends—everything I was able to see just moments ago vanished. Both my eyes had been injured during the explosion. From then on, whenever I encountered hardships, I often thought to myself, "It would have been better if I had perished with my friends."

How was I to overcome this tragedy? The more I thought about it, the more overwhelming it became for me. Probably such hopelessness I felt back then was what led me to study philosophy in later years. "What does it mean to live, and why does war have to happen? For what purpose did I have to become blind to go through all this suffering and hardship?" It made me think deep and hard. From that point on, I began to judge every situation on my own and act accordingly.

The Harsh Refugee Life

I lost my eyesight on a famous farming plantation. The life I lived after a farmer came to tell me that I was still alive was a weary one beyond words. Living in a dark world was truly a tragic life.

The only way to satisfy my extreme thirst was to crawl around the plantation and drink the yellow water collected in the corners of the land. Although I begged and pleaded the passersby to give me some food, hardly anyone did because it was war time. I would run my hands over the field and eat whatever came into my grasp. Sometimes, thinking that I must even eat leaves in order to survive, I ran here and there like a madman.

I heard cannons and tanks mingled with people's shouts and cries. With belongings on their heads and backs, the procession of refugees seemed endless. Soon, I too joined them without any idea of their destination. During our march southward, I suddenly remembered my aunt who had married into a wealthy family in the province of Kyung-Gi, the city of Yang-Ju. I decided to go there. I held onto a glimmer of hope that if I went there, I might be able to cure my blindness and get some education. But how in the world would I find the place? It was by no means a simple task.

My biggest concern was crossing the Han River Bridge which had already been destroyed by the bombing. I promised myself that I would indeed go to Yang-Ju by any means necessary. To keep this promise, I continued with the crowd despite severe hunger pangs. When we arrived at the Han River, there was already a multitude waiting at the edge of the destroyed bridge. The boat could not cross during the day because of the severe bombing; refugees had to steal across secretly during the night. It was impossible for me to set over because of the expensive fare they demanded; however, I hid among the luggage and safely made it across.

Although I succeeded in crossing the river, I sighed at the thought of having to travel over 30 miles to reach my relative's house. But that was my only hope, and I couldn't give up. I dragged my weary body one step at a time. I would crawl, rest a bit, get up and cry my way to my aunt's house. Although it was during war time, and people's compassion had dried up, I was meant to live. There were refugees everywhere, eating meals. When I begged them for food, I always got some because they either found me pitiful or bothersome. Granted the food was cold rice with water and red bean paste, but it melted sweeter than honey in my mouth.

I finally arrived at my aunt's house after many days of struggling and asking many times for directions. Along the way, there were cucumber and melon fields. All the refugees ate all they could and I was also able to get some whenever I asked.

The Contempt I Had to Endure at My Aunt's House

When I finally arrived at my aunt's house, incredibly cruel treatment was waiting for me. Contempt, abuse, hatred—persecution would be a more fitting word. I had to bear all kinds of foul language and curses thrown at me. I was convinced that hell couldn't possibly be any worse than this. Please understand that while I do not want to record everything in detail that had happened to me, I would like to uncover aspects of sinful human nature witnessed by my young bruised spirit. Additionally, all my relatives who have inflicted such pain on me have passed away; I cannot imagine what harm this recollection could possibly bring to them. Also, I hold no resentment toward them. Through the grace of Jesus Christ, I have forgiven their mistakes long ago. Although it is difficult to express in words all the humiliation and abuse I endured, I can still clearly remember the curses and foul language they threw at me.

"Sun-Tae, you are good for nothing, so you should go and either drown yourself or hang yourself. Or it is best to shoot yourself. You should go out and die as you please. Don't ever show up in front of me again!" Or, they would say, "Oxen work because they can see, and dogs can look after the house and are good as food when they die, but I can't give you any work to do, nor eat you. You are nothing more than a food consuming parasite who will never amount to any good in a hundred years, so you should leave this house! The sooner the better!"

Maybe they were ashamed that a blind boy was staying at their house. I couldn't figure out the exact reason. Even my aunt, whom I had trusted completely, mistreated me beyond measure. Despite of it all, I stayed there day after day as I endured their abuse as I had no other option.

The first thing I did when I got up in the morning was to listen to hundreds of venomous curses directed at me. The day started with curses and ended with curses. I never knew there were so many swear words. Such curses thrown at me for the first time in my life tore my innocent heart into pieces. Not only that, my body was purple and blue, completely covered with bruises from beatings I received for no apparent reason. Once my aunt beat me with acacia branches that were used for fire wood. Every time the branch whipped my body, I endured the pain of sharp thorns ripping away my tender flesh. My body still carries some 60 scars that I received at that time.

One day, the entire family accused me of being a thief. This gave them an excuse to beat me mercilessly all at once. 500 *won* hidden in the closet had disappeared, and they accused me of stealing it to buy candy. Of course I denied of ever having done such a thing, but they gave me no chance to explain. Rather, my denials gave them more reason to beat me harder. My aunt scorched my arm with a charcoal stick demanding I tell the truth. Later on, it was discovered the oldest daughter had stolen the money. Bitterly, I was the one who received all the punishment.

That's not all. One time, they again falsely accused me and hit me with a bag containing a hoe, leaving a hole in my skull. Thanks be to God, it healed nicely without being a threat to my life, but the scar remains to this day, clearly visible.

On another occasion, I was given a basketful of beans to peel. As I was busily going about my work, a wooden pillow came flying towards my head, causing me to faint. It hit the right side of my face and ear. I was left deaf in one ear as some liquid discharge oozed out, giving me an unbearable headache and pain throughout the night. The pain was so severe, I was thoroughly convinced it would be the last night of my life. In just a few days however, my injured ear was completely healed. God was at work. Whenever I was slapped to a point that it damaged my ear-drums, God was there to provide whatever healing was necessary.

One day, I was to go out early in the field and drive away birds from eating the grain by screaming and flailing my arms. I was so exhausted at the end of the day, I curled up in the corner of the field and fell asleep. When I awoke, I was so hungry; so I ate some of the grain, and drank the water collected in the corner of the field. That day, I was severely beaten for eating grain. Thinking back now, my aunt's family was Buddhist just as my family was. They were very superstitious. If someone ever got sick, I became the first target of vengeance. They said "It's because blind Sun-Tae brings us bad luck!"; then they lashed out their curses and beat me severely.

There is yet another incident I cannot forget. Whenever there were guests, they always locked me in the backyard storage area. They would have all the neighbors as well as distant relatives together and have a big party. When they were done, they would bring me out close to sundown. As I stayed in the storage room all day, my intestines twisted into knots as the smell of wonderful food overwhelmed my senses. The abuse was to an extent that a neighborhood elderly lady had pity on me and gave me flour cakes made with potatoes and beans along with a drink made of sweetened rice. "Eat this and live well. May heaven help you. This household will come to ruin for sure. They don't know the old saying that if they treat disabled children well, they will be blessed!" In such a way, she comforted me on several different occasions.

The Night of Terror

On a sweltering August summer afternoon in 1950, I was sitting on the edge of the wooden floor, peeling beans as ordered by my aunt's mother-in-law (I will call her 'Grandmother' for convenience). I had been peeling the entire morning and my fingers felt like they were falling off. For lunch, I was given a ball of brown rice with some cold cucumber soup. It was simply delicious.

After the meal, Grandmother told me to carry an A-frame, a wooden contraption designed to carry logs and heavy objects on one's back, and to follow her. She had some pumpkins she wanted me to carry. I felt lost. I had never carried an A-frame let alone seen one. But now, I had to carry the heavy load of pumpkins placed on the A-frame on my back. If I had said no, I was afraid of the beating as well as missing a meal, so I did as I was told.

I was a ten-year-old boy of small physique. When I lifted the A-frame made for adults, it dragged on the ground. It was difficult to manage with my limited strength. Seeing this, the daughter of the household tightened the ropes for me. I followed Grandmother through the fields, over the streams, for a considerable distance. Grandmother told me, "Follow the sound of my footsteps" and she took the lead. Since people wore moccasins back then, it made quite a noise.

We finally arrived at the pumpkin field. The other family members were already there packaging the melons they had picked for wholesale. The sweet smell of melons tempted me greatly, but I wasn't even offered one for tasting.

Close to nightfall, my A-frame was full of pumpkins they had picked. As I tried to get up with the full A-frame on my back, I fell back at the sheer weight of the pumpkins. Grandmother proceeded to kick me as she yelled, "Can't you even lift this? You should at least earn your own rice!" Tears poured out uncontrollably.

Grandfather and other uncles of the household all agreed, "Sun-Tae should be thrown out!" They started to drag me away. They told me to grab onto the cart drawn by a cow and to follow them. After the sun set, I had no idea where we were. They stopped the cart in front of a little hut and told me, "You live here from now on." They put me inside the hut and left.

'Where is this? Is this an abandoned house? Who lives here?' I wondered to myself. I felt strange objects as I groped in the dark. I heard the purring of cats and swarms of mosquitoes. There were wolves and foxes in the forest then. No matter how much I felt around, it felt strange. I stumbled a few steps forward and soon found a large bamboo tree. I was so scared that I climbed the tree. The branches forked out into three directions. I spent that night alone in terror and trembling between the branches. Near dawn, I heard people passing by as the bells on the ox pierced sharply through the dense air. I thought, 'Now I'll be okay', and yelled out to a passerby, "Mister, please help me. Where am I?"

The farmer was shocked, "Where did you come from? Why are you here? This is where they place the dead before burial," he replied. 'That's why it felt so eerie last night,' I thought to myself. The farmer asked me whether I had spent the night here and sympathized with me. He brought me down from the tree and asked me to follow him by holding onto his cart. After traveling for some time, we came across farmers' wives bringing out lunch to their husbands working in the field. The farmer gave me a bowl of white and brown rice mixed with pickles and fermented radish with hot pepper paste. It melted on my tongue. I had never tasted such delicious mixed rice in my entire life.

The farmer asked me once again how I had ended up in a place like that. I only told him that I was being punished for not doing my work well. After lunch, the farmer took me to my aunt's house. At the first glimpse of me, my aunt yelled at me, "How come you weren't devoured by the ghosts there? Now that the farmer has brought you back, how are we to live with such shame!" She took me to an isolated room and beat me mercilessly. Just thinking about it makes me shiver even now.

Maybe I Should Just Die

September was a time of confusion and violence. The sound of bombs and guns were constantly in the air, and people were seeking refuge in anti-Communist shelters. Communists invaded houses and ransacked everything. But even in that chaos, my aunt's house celebrated *Chusok* (equivalent to a Korean Thanksgiving) by making flour cakes, and slaughtering chicken for soup. The entire family gathered on the wooden floor, enjoying their meal. My aunt took me to the backyard and told me to stay very still until all the relatives were gone. Being a fearful boy, I did exactly as I was told for hours on end.

I could hear them talking and laughing as the dog kept going back and forth. I was waiting for them to call me in to give me some meat soup and tasty flour cakes. After a while, Grandmother called me. 'Now, they are going to give me something to eat!' I went to the front porch full of excitement. But contrary to my expectations, they ordered me to do an impossible task. Grandmother gave me a large sickle to go and cut grass to feed the cows. Finding my way to the grassland was a secondary concern; I had never handled a sickle in my life! But to get fed, I had to do as I was told. There was a mountain if you went straight from the house. The place was known to be full of snakes hiding in the dense woods.

I was to carry back a full load of grass on the A-frame if I wanted to receive any food. Although I had no confidence I could actually cut down the grass with a sickle, I had to try. In my futile attempt, I cut my left index finger. It wouldn't stop bleeding. I took a leaf from a tall oak tree and wrapped it around my finger until the bleeding stopped. I was starving and felt bitterly sorry for myself. I thought that it would be better to die than live like this. I took off my belt and started to choke myself. At that moment, I heard a strange voice, "Don't die! There will come a day when you will grow up and put this behind you." It was so strange; I stopped the suicide attempt.

The sun had set. Grandmother and my cousin came to get me, but when she saw I had not cut down a single blade of grass, she grabbed a branch and started beating me as if to kill me. I screamed for help but no one came. My forearm and calves swelled up. After she finished beating me, she brought me back home.

She sat me down on the floor and gave me rice in water with a scanty ration of flour cakes. My aunt and Grandmother sat on the edge of the floor and cursed that I might choke to death with each spoonful as they alternately took turns punching my head. I had to endure the abuse because I was so hungry. After I finished eating, with tears dripping down my face, I promised I would take my own life that night.

During the deep night, with everyone fast asleep, I went to the well in the front yard and immersed my face in the water. I tried to fall in headfirst. The water engulfed my forehead and the deed would have been finished in a moment as my eyes, nose and mouth were nearing the pool of water. But the voice came again, "Endure this. Get yourself out of the well. I will help you." It felt as if someone was pulling my feet to the ground. I gave up trying to drown myself.

The finger injured by the sickle was infected and started to swell. The pain was unbearable. Fortunately, there was an elderly man in the town who, seeing my finger, diagnosed it as poisonous swelling. To eliminate the poison from my finger, he took some herbs, set them on fire and scorched my finger with them. The pain left a scar on my left index. The elderly man continued the treatment for several days. If he had not given me the herbal treatment, the poison would have spread and the finger would have been amputated, leaving me without a finger to read Braille in the days to come.

The Conspiracy to Kill a Blind Nephew

Summer and autumn passed, and winter arrived with a vengeance. The winter of 1950 was colder and snowed more than any other. The war continued and I was as tired as a rag. I could not sleep in a warm room for a single night. I had to spread a woven bag of hay on the wooden floor and sleep with a rice bag as my blanket. One night, it was so cold, I slept with my feet inside the lit furnace.

During the December of 1950, refugees were on the move. The night before our departure, something horrible almost happened to me. It wasn't easy for my aunt's family to leave behind all the rice and chestnuts they had harvested, but their primary concern was disposal of a blind nephew.

"In order to look after our possessions, let's have the old people stay while the younger ones leave. And since we can't have Sun-Tae come with us nor stay behind, we will mix the leftover alkaline solution from our laundry into his breakfast rice and kill him off. When he dies, we will bury him in the woods and be on our way." When I had overheard their conversation, the will to live dominated my mind. I decided to escape. While everyone was sleeping, I stole away and ran as fast as my legs would carry me. Thus, I was back where I had started.

The Exodus of My Life: *"Get Up and Leave This Place"*

Although I had grown up in a devout Buddhist family, I regularly attended Sunday school despite the opposition from my parents and grandmother. So in the midst of the abuse and humiliation I had to endure at my aunt's house, I did not lose my faith and hope. I learned to pray whenever I came across hardship in my life. I knelt down and prayed with all my might on the night of my exodus.

"Heavenly Father! If you will let me live, I will become a great person in the future. I want to live my life for those who are blind like me." My prayer was truly desperate and sincere. When I prayed that prayer, I heard a voice within me, "Sun-Tae! Don't worry. I love you. Leave this place. I will lead you."

Just as Moses took the people of Israel out of Egypt, I stepped into the darkness of the night with my shoes, rice bag on my back and a staff in my hand. I began my own Exodus. Oh, that scary and trembling night! I climbed the mountain, crossed the river and ran with all my strength toward the main street. As I passed through a valley of various tombs scattered here and there, I could feel the presence of wolves and foxes. Although my entire body was frozen with cold, my back, hands and feet felt warm. It was truly strange; it was the presence of God's love.

As I walked, I sang the song I learned in an attempt to drive away fear.

> *Jesus is our bright light.*
> *He says to us as He shines,*
> *'You are the light of the world,*
> *You are the light of the world!'*

I calmed down when I reached the main street. Out of fear of being caught by my aunt's family, I kept pace with the rest of the war refugees heading South. I felt like the Israelites being chased by the Egyptian army. It was a long and endless journey. My feet were swollen and my body exasperated. However, what made me sad was that I had nobody waiting for me. I was a lonely leaf floating in the midst of a great crowd of war refugees.

When I think back to that time, my body cringes in horror. "Oh Lord, why did you make me suffer so much? Was it because without such hardship I would never have endured the challenging ministry for the visually disabled? Thank you for giving me the faith in resurrection through the hellish training I received."

The distance I had covered as a ten year old boy that night would probably equal 16 to 20 miles. That night, I made a firm decision: Whatever happened, I would never depend on or return to my relative's family. That decision helped me in the future to easily leave a place in faith where I couldn't feel comfortable. I am assured now that I owe all my triumph over desperate situations to the lesson I had learned on that cold, frightful night of December 22, 1950. To make me the light and salt of this world, God took away my parents, my relatives, and my brothers and sisters. He made me into a man who possessed absolutely nothing. If we want to live the life of Jesus and His disciples, a life of total destitution, we should first have a heart of gratitude for being called and chosen to live the life of self-denial, carrying a cross, and following Him.

If I had not triumphed over my wasted life through faith during the Korean War, I would have never attempted to learn the spiritual discipline that arose from poverty and pain. I can see from my own experience how hard it is for the wealthy to enter the kingdom of God. Had I not experienced a life of grace as I lived in persecution and hunger, I would have never known the true meaning of spiritual discipline that drew me closer to Christ. Just as the Israelites escaped from a life of oppression and slavery to face the treacherous desert life, I started on a journey of my own in the midst of the grueling Korean War. The two years during which I wandered to and from various cities in Korea were truly a miraculous time in my life. "Lord, thank you for your grace which taught me the power of salvation through an exodus such as that of the Israelites.

The Heroes I Met in the Desert

On the Train to Seoul

My "exodus" wasn't by any means hopeful or glorious; it was a road of loneliness and pain. I was the pitiful image of the "King of the Beggars". At least I was sheltered at my aunt's house before, but since the exodus, I constantly battled with foul weather and hunger. It wasn't easy being a beggar in Pusan where the streets were lined with beggars. I thought about going back to Seoul where it was easier to beg. The problem was, how was a beggar supposed to get to Seoul? I needed to buy a train ticket but had no way of obtaining any money; I decided to go anyway.

I secretly boarded the train. Whenever the train master came around, I hid under the seat, or a passenger would hide me in the bathroom. However, near the destination, a problem arose. Since it was wartime, everyone needed a pass to cross the Han River. Young boys weren't allowed to cross, so I had to disembark at Young Deung Po Station, the station before Seoul. I continued to beg there. Since I was somewhat used to living a beggar's life, I had no problem living from day to day.

From the King of Beggars to a Gentleman

During my time at Young Deung Po Station, I met an American soldier. The only English I knew was "Hello", "Help me", "Please give me", and "Thank you". I gathered all my courage and approached the American. I said, "Please help me." The young man immediately took me to his place and gave me hot chocolate, socks and some undergarments.

This first act of kindness I had encountered in my life moved me. Although I was already impressed at how the blue-eyed soldiers were fighting for our country, what impressed me even more was the kindness they showed me. I was instantaneously transformed from the king of beggars to a gentleman. The kind soldier called around to find me a place in the Italian hospital near a local elementary school. The wounded king of beggars was finally being treated with kindness for the first time in his life. Not only was every wound treated during my two months of stay at the hospital, I was eating like a real king. I was in heaven.

The Days Spent in the Sam Eh Orphanage

After receiving treatment at the hospital, the American soldier took me to the Sam-Eh Orphanage. I thanked God for the kind American soldier I had met in the desert and expressed my gratitude to the soldier a hundred times over. The orphanage was a Buddhist temple before the war, but it was now being used as a shelter for 300 orphans. Although it was a well-run orphanage which provided me with three hot meals a day and clean place to sleep, I had a serious problem. All the children beat me up and made fun of me. Additionally, I wasn't able to attend the elementary school like the rest of the kids. The joy at finding a place of rest was soon replaced as my sorrow increased day by day. I envied my friends' studies. My desire to study was so great, I left the orphanage after six weeks of searching for a place that would allow me to study. Before I left, however, I met with the orphanage head and thanked him for all his kindness.

The clothes given to me by the American soldier and the clothes I received from the orphanage improved my appearance, but begging in those clothes was difficult. Instead of having pity on me, people threw offensive remarks at me and accused me of trying to rip them off. Then high-ranking beggars took my clothes and left me with filthy rags. I was back where I started. I did the best I could, begging in the most popular spots. No words can describe the obstacles I faced, the humiliations endured, or the tragedies experienced begging in the midst of a war.

One day, after finishing off the day's begging, I teamed up with my fellow beggars to find shelter. We entered an abandoned house but left immediately because decaying bodies were everywhere. Such horrors were not rare in those days.

My Encounter with an American Army Chaplain

I encountered an American army chaplain in the midst of my wandering beggar days. He took me to his platoon, gave me a bath and new clothes to wear, then took me to an orphanage of 400-500 children run by a Methodist pastor. The chaplain visited me every two weeks and brought chocolate, cookies and pastries whenever he came. He taught me a word or two of English per visit. Thinking back now, I owe my fluency in English to that army chaplain.

The orphanage was not insulated and therefore, freezing cold during the winter. Although they had a small coal furnace in each dorm room, it never produced enough heat for 20 or 30 kids to sleep warmly. Sometimes, the kids in the upper room would urinate in their sleep and the urine would drip in the mouth or face of those sleeping in the lower rooms.

The food was much worse than my previous orphanage. A typical meal consisted of a bowl of brown rice with salt soup. In addition to poor food, the cafeteria was so cold that the food would turn frosty by the time the server brought it to the table. I had no doubt that I had to flee that orphanage as well. Within three months of my arrival, a visitor gave me news about an orphanage for the disabled. He told me they provided an education appropriate to my disability. It was delightful news for me. I begged him to take me there. I received permission from the orphanage superintendent and was transferred.

The Pitiful War Orphans

The Horizon Orphanage was a gathering place for children with all types of disabilities. Some had epilepsy, some had their legs amputated, some were paraplegics, some dumb and mute, some had mental retardation, and the list went on. There were about 200 of us. I remember being the only blind child. It was a difficult situation for me to bear.

The Horizon Orphanage was a zoo-like; the animals were all wild or mad. Some of the scenes I witnessed in my mind petrified me. Unassisted, epilepsy patients would go into seizures and foam at the mouth. Mentally retarded children would eat their own feces. The mentally insane ran with scissors threatening to kill all of us. It was common for stronger children to steal others' food during meals. Even the teachers in charge must have snapped because they often beat children with clubs for no apparent reason. Shocked by such scenes, I realized this wasn't a place for me. I decided to run away. I realized that there were many war orphans who were even worse off than I was. This thought brought comfort and encouragement to me. I came to the realization that I was too healthy of body and mind to be self-abusive, self-loathing and condemning of the world.

The Plan to Escape From the Horizon Orphanage

One day, I promised my friend Jung-Woon Kim, who had a bullet wound on his right foot that we would escape together from the orphanage. We were afraid that if we stayed, we would become more handicapped than ever. Although we had a plan to escape, we didn't know where to go. We decided on Choonchun, a place we heard others talk about when we were begging. Choonchun was mostly occupied by American GI's, which made it ideal for begging. Remembering back, I believe American soldiers were the closest and most gracious friends of the war orphans.

The night of our escape arrived. The blind boy and limping beggar secretly stole away in the dead of night and started on their long and tumultuous journey. We thought if we went back to Seoul we might get caught. So we boarded an American army truck headed for Choonchun. We succeeded in our midnight flight.

A few hours after our success, there was an inspection. We needed travel permits to go to Choonchun, but we didn't have any form of identification. The GI who allowed us to ride in his truck took us to his shelter and gave us warm chocolate milk to drink while we thawed out. He asked a fellow soldier to take us to Seoul.

We didn't get to Choonchun as we wanted, but were shipped back to Seoul on another truck. When we arrived, the American gave us a couple of dollars and some food. With the money, we headed to buy train tickets to Pusan, and headed there without further ado.

I believe it was because of the numerous trials and suffering I endured in life that allowed me to possess such a strong sense of purpose and vision for my life. What after all is the basic message of the Bible? Isn't it the proclamation of grace to those who are poor and sick? Those brothers and sisters who are carrying out the work of Christ by embodying His grace and love should be reminded constantly that they are simply instruments through whom God is proclaiming His message. My short life was so turbulent, I couldn't expect any satisfactory results from the seemingly endless and grueling desert life of mine. Nevertheless, I never ceased to offer up prayers to my Good Shepherd.

The Pauper Prince in the Kingdom of Beggars

The Kind Neighbors of the Beggar Community

There were several times that I thought I was a Pauper Prince. There is, of course, a hierarchy even in the beggar world. A tight order existed in this beggardom. Territorial and authority divisions were very distinct among all the beggars. In Pusan, my territory covered an area from the train station to the fish market. I often slept on or underneath the boards merchants left behind after a day of hard work. I could usually sleep there undisturbed by those looking to cart away beggars like me.

There were kind merchant women who sold food at discounted prices to the beggar community. They were the main figures in our community. The best reward for a beggar is food. Early in the morning, beggars with empty tin cans would go in search of nice women merchants. The beggars would ask nicely in Kyung-Sang Province dialect, "Please give us a bowl of food." Sometimes, the women gave food, sometimes they didn't. It depended on their mood.

But whenever I came, they always gave me a full can of food. Some women would say, "You know, I didn't even have my first sale for the day, but why don't you eat this food and grow strong." They would comfort me with such words. Other women complimented my nose—that it was so good looking, a sign of future blessing. Although I went hungry many times, I was happy to share in the fellowship of my neighbor. After eating a tin can of hot stew, the task of begging in the international market made up the rest of my day.

Evangelizing to the Errand Boys

There was an invisible hierarchy among the beggars recognized regardless of where you went. There were four ranks in beggardom with the chief being the highest and the errand boys the lowest. Before I knew it, I had reached the highest rank among the beggars. I became a chief beggar in Pusan because I earned good money. Not only that, I knew how to be generous to other beggars. A chief also needed strong character. As word got out that whoever messed with me was dead meat, I had about ten small errand boys following me. I didn't miss this chance to evangelize.

I had an opportunity to share Christ with others for the first time with the errand boys who were very happy to go to church with me. "Whoever goes to church with me will get money, 'pig stew' and even yummy pastries!" I would tempt them. If any one of them memorized John 3:16, "For God so loved the world, He gave His one and only begotten Son that whosoever believes in Him shall not perish but have everlasting life," I would reward them handsomely with delicious pastries. Of course, the 'pig stew' was the ultimate reward.

'Pig stew' was leftover food from the American army base that was gathered and sold off to markets. The markets would put everything together and make what we called 'pig stew'. Sometimes chicken or fish bones would pop up in the stew, but for beggars, it was one of the best dishes ever. We would eat anything. Inedible food was often given out by inns or marketplaces. Though not often, we would sometimes find used tissues or chewed food in the stew. I never failed to thank God for the food I received.

The best part of my promotion to chief was that I could sleep in privileged places like under the bridge, or next to a chimney of someone's house without having to worry about other beggars kicking me out. Other beggars knew better than to mess with me. Even though I was a chief beggar, I went to church every Sunday. I choose the newest bill from the money I had earned for the offering. Some churches would try to drag me out and give me a couple of coins, but I never yielded when it came to worshipping God on Sundays.

The Chief Beggar Gets a Cold Reception at Church

Whatever church I would go to, I tried hard not to lose my princely attitude for I indeed knew I was a prince in the heavenly kingdom. Even though the churches treated me like a beggar come to beg and often kicked me out, I did not argue with them. Like royalty, I moved on to a different church in the neighborhood. I wonder if today's church still makes the mistake of mistreating little Christs who appear in the form of a beggar. Whenever I think of my own experience, it saddens me greatly.

Sometimes, I would be poisoned with lacquer; my body would be completely covered with watery discharges from all my sores. I believed I had to go to church on Sundays. When I went, they would treat me like a leper and kick me out. In their eyes, I was only a poor beggar, but I waited patiently for the day I would show them my true self. Although they would throw stones and dirt at me calling me a 'leper beggar', I forgave them and even offered up a prayer on their behalf.

A Pauper Prince with Lacquer Poisoning

For a beggar, wherever he went was his home, wherever he slept was his bedroom, and whoever gave him money was his brother, sister, or mother. During the night, stacks of wheat, corn, or beanstalks served as an ideal place to lean against comfortably and keep out the wind.

I had traveled to a certain town in Cholla Province and after a good day of begging, I found a shack full of tree trunks. I did not know they were lacquer trees. After sleeping there, my body started to itch from head to toe. Rashes appeared all over my body. "What could this be? Maybe a mouse has bitten me, or fleas." I contemplated over the rash. I left it alone for a few days but as time went by, the pain increased and pus began to flow from the sores. It felt like my skin was rotting away. Begging in that condition only got stones thrown at me and buckets of water poured on me because they thought I was a leper. Some houses even let their hunting dogs loose after me so that I would never come back.

The pain was becoming unbearable. The poison had spread to my organs so that my stomach was bloated and I could hardly walk. My voice was gone, and if I pressed my face, it went in like a lump of flour dough. I was miserable.

One morning sitting under a tree, I was crying aloud blaming everything on the war, when I heard an elderly lady pass singing a hymn. When she saw me, she exclaimed, "Oh no! You have been poisoned with lacquer! The poison has spread to your organs. What should we do? Give me your hand." She grabbed my smelly, watery hand and started to pray for me.

"Lord, please let this boy live and heal him from this poisoning."

After praying fervently, she said, "Don't despair. Even if everyone in this world forsakes you, Jesus loves you. God will help you." And so she encouraged me and went on her way.

I regained my courage. 'There is still such a person in this wicked world who will hold my hand,' I thought. I sat there for two hours as I thought about such things. Surprisingly, the elderly woman came back, looking for me. "I was worried you might have gone somewhere else. Let's go to my house. I couldn't do anything at home because I kept thinking about you. I believe you must be an angel sent to me by God." And she took me to her home. Entering her house, she took off my ragged clothes and gave me a bath in chicken stock. After praying for me, she used her own mouth to suck out the poison from my face and arms. How grateful I was!

For over twenty days, she took good care of me. She helped me all she could. I was healed completely of the smelly, itchy lacquer poisoning. When healed, the elderly lady told me, "I have a son who was drafted to war. I don't know whether he is dead or alive. Although I have some fields, since I can't farm by myself, I barely survive with the help of my neighbors. If only I had money, I would let you live with me, fix your eyes, and make you into God's servant, but I am powerless. However, I will always pray for you until my dying moment. May you go all over the world and become an instrument of love, spreading the good news of Christ everywhere you go!" After praying for me, she sent me away in tears. I imagined her standing outside watching me go until I vanished from sight.

She is probably praying for me in heaven. Because of that elderly lady's power of love, I was able to become God's servant. How could I ever forget her warm loving touch! After that incident, whenever I faced difficult situations, I would remind myself of the comfort I had received then and take it as proof of God's love for me. If it wasn't for God's grace, how could I have ever survived through the war? There were many beggar boys around. Although they were healthy beggars with two eyes, they still died of food poisoning, or airplane raids, froze, or starved to death. Even though we walked through the same valley of death, this chief beggar, or rather this Pauper Prince, survived as robustly and courageously as ever.

The Reason to Live

One spring afternoon, after my fellow beggars and I went around town and had lunch, we arrived at a small hill behind a wealthy house. Some of us sat on the grass while others dozed off as they stretched themselves out comfortably. I sat and thought about the life I had lived, wondering how I should live from now on. 'When will this life of beggary come to an end? Isn't it too meaningless to live and die like this? Will there come a day when I can see the world with my own eyes?' I thought about such things although I knew deep down that I was only fooling myself.

I gazed toward the sun with my blind eyes, then fixed my eyes on the field. Uncontrollable tears wet my face. 'Where will I eat and sleep tonight? What if I meet a beggar who is more experienced than I and get beaten up? What if a dog bites me? Maybe I should just climb up a big tree in the middle of the night and kill myself. Or, maybe I should throw myself into the river and drown.' Each thought plunged me deeper and deeper into despair.

The sun had set, and my beggar companions wanted to go back to town and beg for dinner. Just then, handfuls of some wildflowers and blossoming azaleas came into my grasp. These flowers lifted me from the pit of depression. They completely changed my mind. If God gives new life to even the flowers and grass which have withered away during the winter, how much more would God do for his own masterpiece like me? I am definitely better than a blade of grass! Why should I despair when all I have lost is my eyesight? I still had my life. I couldn't stay disheartened when I knew I was more precious than any withering flower or blades of grass. I grabbed my tin can and prayed, "Lord, just as the field and trees are budding, let hope also bud within my heart."

Even now, when spring arrives and I see the budding trees and the flowers, I am reminded of that day in the field and the things I had thought in tears. The prayer I offered then has been answered fully and I am now a dedicated leader in God's church and society. I cannot forget the lesson God taught me through nature that day in the field. Hope comes from despair; light comes from darkness. Wealth and happiness come from poverty and misfortunes. Dreams and hopes are seeds to wealth and happiness.

The Chief Beggar's Early
School Years

Caught by the Warrant to Arrest all Beggars

As I was getting used to life as a beggar, the order went out to gather all beggars into one place and divide them up to be sent to orphanages or prisons. I had to leave my carefree life behind and be subject to governmental rules. This was one of the social undertakings ordered by the City of Pusan.

Roaming the back alleys of the international marketplace, someone appeared and forcefully threw away my tin can and dragged me into a van. They had already collected about 45 others. The van was a horror to every beggar. 'They are probably taking me someplace to kill me right now.' Such thoughts gave me a chill; my body trembled like a leaf.

Thankfully, we were taken to a children's shelter. It was a temporary prison where they gathered all the beggars and educated them before placing them into different orphanages. The building had twelve divisions and there were about 100 people per division. Orphans were divided depending on their past behavior. Troublemakers would be sent away to desolate islands, while those with relatively good behavior would be assigned to nice orphanages.

We had worship every week at the children's shelter. I was assigned to Division 4 because of my good behavior. Only good kids were allowed to go to Division 4. They evaluated the orphans and sent them to different islands or orphanages every three weeks. One day, the superintendent and the director of the children's shelter came and asked me to what orphanage I wished to be sent. Isabel Orphanage and the New Prairie Orphanage in Pusan were known to be exemplary orphanages. They were unique orphanages where the staff didn't beat you and allowed you to worship on Sundays. However, I clearly stated my intention to study. I figured that an orphanage that would allow me to study would also allow me to worship. After a few days, the superintendent and the director called me into the office. They wrote me a recommendation to a school for the blind called The Light House.

Memories of the Light House: The School for the Blind

Three days later, I was in a car, headed toward the Light House in Song Do Valley. When I arrived, there were 150 other blind children. I would begin my new life with them. With the recommendation from the children's shelter in hand, I went to the second floor office. A short, friendly man gave me a warm greeting. After asking me several questions, he remarked that I was very smart and said, "Study hard at our facility so that you may become a prominent person who fulfills his dreams." He was Rev. Duk-Hong Lee, the principal of the Light House School for the Blind. He was a respected social worker who had established the Seoul School for the Blind along with the Light House.

However, elementary children could not remain in Seoul. I had to be transferred to the Light House branch in Kim-Hae. Many of my friends who were transferred with me at that time, have long been deceased. The only remaining teacher from the Light House is Elder Yong-Bong Park of Namsan Baptist Church. It is said he lost his eyesight while teaching math at Korea University. The long deceased Mrs. Han was the head teacher for the younger blind children and Elder Park was the head teacher for the older children. Mrs. Han went to be with the Lord after serving as superintendent and principal of One Light School for the Blind. I was able to run errands, and clean up for Mrs. Han who was more like a mother than a teacher. I could never forget the way she loved she me like a mother would her child.

After learning to read Korean Braille, we had our first summer break. In Kim-Hae, there were apple and pear orchards, grape fields, persimmon fields, and plenty of fruit to eat. As soon as the early morning class let out, we would go swimming in the nearby river. The memory of stealing some grapes from the field and rinsing them in the river seems like only yesterday.

We found thrill and excitement in stealing away to persimmon trees in the middle of the night and eating them, or stealing some potatoes and eating them with teachers and friends. We would make crab stew with what the older kids caught in the river. At night, we would sit in the ship warehouse, talking and eating roasted corn and potatoes. Oh, how I miss those days sitting in front of the bonfire as we regretfully felt the delicious summer slipping away.

But those happy times only lasted for one summer. In the fall, 150 students were shipped back to the School for the Blind in Seoul. The younger students from Kim-Hae were taken back to the Light House in Song-Do, which was the headquarter for handicapped schools at that time with over 100 deaf and mute students and only 50 blind students. Because I had learned Braille well, I was transferred into the 4th grade, and after only a semester, I was able to enter the 6th grade.

Hurts from Discrimination and Misunderstanding

I had to endure a year and a half of pure torture at that place. There were numerous cruel experiences I had to face. At the time, the Light House staff would mercilessly beat the blind students. Even the teachers joined in the cruel treatment toward the students. Also, Teacher Han would drink all night, burst into students' rooms early in the morning, demanding a massage. It didn't end there. He would enter the girls' rooms in the middle of the night, performing acts which were completely inappropriate for a teacher. The worst of the ordeal was that no one cared enough to put a stop to any of the abuses. I felt a great deal of emotional distress during those days. Is this what schools for the handicapped are really like? Could these people really be called teachers?

One evening, the teachers' gathering was almost coming to an end. When they got up to go, one of teacher Yoo's shoestrings was missing. The next day, the dorm supervisor, Mr. Yang, called me into his office. He accused me of stealing Teacher Yoo's shoestring and tortured me for the next two hours with a bamboo stick. What would I possibly do with a female teacher's shoestring? Even though many of the students could see my swollen legs, they were too fearful to say anything. There is still a living witness to what had happened that morning. Tears moisten my eyes even at this very moment as I'm penning the event.

But that wasn't the last time Mr. Yang gave me such pain. New Year's Day of 1954, all the teachers and students were enjoying themselves eating rice soup (a traditional Korean dish eaten on New Year's Day) and playing a game of *yut* (a traditional New Year's game played with five sticks). However, the topic of the conversation soon turned to the future of each student in the room. The teachers started to critique each student's abilities and potential. Mr. Yang, however, only complimented those students who had given him presents or were nice to him, saying they showed great promise. He looked at me and said that I had no hope whatsoever. "Since you don't study and only goof around all the time, you will be lucky if you graduate from this school and get a job as a masseur."

I held in my blood boiling anger and ran from the room. There was a staircase of 70 steps in the soldiers' apartment complex about 500 meters from the school where we often visited to play, sing and feel the shore breeze graze our faces.

I was so upset and angry, I started praying in tears. "Am I really as hopeless as Mr. Yang says?" That night, I heard the gracious voice of God in the lapping of the waves. I stood up in utter amazement. "Don't worry. I have overcome the world. You are my beloved child. I will help you." The voice gave me the courage to decide within my heart to attend a regular school.

When I returned, Mr. Yang interrogated me as to why I was outside for so long. I honestly answered that I had been praying and went to sleep. I feared Mr. Yang would physically abuse me again in the morning. I went to Elder Kun Ho Lee, the superintendent, and told him the story. I also told him that if Mr. Yang stayed, I would have to leave the school. His wife comforted me with tears in her eyes. Since she was already aware of his crimes, she said she would be taking action soon. Not long after that, Mr. Yang was transferred to the Kim-Hae Women's School for the Blind.

The Masseur

I cannot continue without relating another episode that took place while I was at the Pusan Light House. One day, Teacher Lee called me and made me an offer. "How would you like to earn some pocket money by going out to the city and giving massages?" That got me excited. I said yes, I would like to try it very much. There was a particular hotel in Song-Do which was occupied by many American and Japanese visitors. It was also a very busy area because of the American Army base.

One day in 1954, I went to the hotel to give a massage for the first time in my life. The American client's body was so big, it felt like a hard tree trunk. I did my best for an hour. My client kept repeating "wonderful!" Afterwards he opened a can of Coke and offered it to me, he requested that I give a massage to his female companion who was with him for another hour. When I received the pay from him, I realized it was double the amount of a regular massaging fee.

The next day, after setting aside money for church offering, I sent over a few pounds of beef to the teacher who had introduced me to the job. That very day, I heard the news that his father-in-law had passed away. I gave him the remainder of my money to be used for funeral costs.

Shortly after, Teacher Lee called again and suggested that I do massaging regularly so that I would have enough money saved up for my middle school tuition. Even though there was a danger of being beaten close to death if my upper classmates found out that a lower classman had taken a better work position, the teacher kept introducing me to the hotels. He told me that all the responsibility would be on his shoulders and encouraged me to earn as much money as I could during the summer.

He even gave me a bamboo flute. Back in those days, a flute was the lifeline to many blind people. Whenever I went around residential areas or hotels, playing my flute, they would shout out, "it's the masseur!" Every night around 9:00 pm, I walked around the Song-Do shore area playing my flute. Since the area was a well-known spot for tourists, many blind people came from all over the place to earn money as masseurs. Although I was shy and embarrassed at first, I soon gained confidence and courage.

On good nights, I would have about four customers and on bad nights, I would have only one. The money I earned over the summer was the most money I had ever touched up to that point in my life. Of course, I gave a tenth of my earnings to the church. Towards the end of summer, the touring season ended on the shores of Song-Do. By then there was also no money left in my pockets. Due to my lack of greed, I had spent all my money on tasty pastries and treating my friends.

There was one lesson I had learned during my massaging days. Although I had mastered the massaging techniques, thanks to Mr. Yang who had demanded my service every night, I had promised myself to never to become a full-time masseur. The cocktail parties and sexual activities that took place in hotel rooms where I gave out massages frightened me. I was afraid that I, too, would fall into such temptations if I were to make a living out of massaging.

During my days at the Pusan School for the Handicapped, I often studied with the deaf and mute students. Of course, the deaf and mute studied separately through sign language. The school also taught us sign language so that we could study together for tests. However, the teachers complimented the blind students on our higher test scores. There were many times the blind students were made objects of mockery among the deaf and mute students because we would constantly run into things and frequently fall down.

Hanyang Church

I can remember 1955 as the year when the great revival took place in the surrounding city of Pusan. At the time, the area had become cluttered with all the refugees from Pyung-Ahn and Ham-Kyung Province. Included in this crowd were believers from Ham-Heung and Wonsan who had taken refuge in Pusan.

One day, Rev. Soon-Jik Choi and Evangelist Myung-Sook Lee visited our school. I was playing in the playground when they approached. They asked me, "Do you believe in Jesus? Do you believe in John chapter 9?" I vividly remember answering, "Yes, I believe John chapter 9 with all of my heart and I also believe that God will heal my eyes." From then on, Reverend Choi recommended me to attend Hanyang Church. I experienced great love from that church. They would throw love feasts whenever the blind students attended the service. Also, my faith was strengthened greatly through the church. Three blind students who attended the church during that time became pastors, including myself.

Orphans and widows inevitably increased because of the Korean war. I believe the revival movements were effective in strengthening and disciplining the minds of powerless refugees.

There was a particular individual by the name of Elder Tae-Sun Park who rose up like the glorious morning sun, comforting those who had completely lost hope. Hundreds of people gathered in the Pusan Stadium for a revival meeting that continued day and night for ten days. Although we were just kids, we walked all the way to the Pusan Stadium after hearing all the amazing miracles he had supposedly performed. After praying all night, we would return to school early in the morning, and when school was over, we would go right back to the revival meeting.

We wanted to be prayed for by Elder Park, so we waited in line all night long. As Elder Park passed by us, we would stick our heads out so that he might touch us with his powerful hand. But at the end of the night, we were as blind as ever. The lady next to us rebuked us, "It's because you boys don't have enough faith. I suggest you guys stay here overnight praying, and in the morning, when he passes by you, grab onto his arm and beg for healing."

Being as naive as I was, I did as she told us even if it meant missing school. After the all night prayer meeting came the early prayer time when Elder Park went around praying for people making a wind-like noise with his lips. My turn finally came. I mustered up enough courage to grab onto his arm, and with all my strength I pleaded him, "Please, Elder Park, open my eyes!"

His arm felt like a sturdy wooden pillar. But unexpectedly, he punched me in the cheek. His fist was strong enough to have deafened me for life. In an attempt to heal my eyes, I had almost become deaf as well! Only then did I realize that he was a fake. I immediately got up and headed back to school. Through that night, I was assured more than ever that God had special plans for me, just as I was.

B
O
O
K

II

Spiritual Discipline from
the School of
the Wilderness

Dreaming of a Flight
to the New World

Where There is a Will, There is a Way

It was the winter break of 1955. I decided that there was nothing left for me to learn at the Pusan School and thought how nice it would be to study at the Seoul School for the Blind. As soon as school was out for the winter, I threw myself onto a train for Seoul. I was determined to find the Seoul School for the Blind, a school I had never visited before. I got off at the Seoul Train Station. Without a warm winter coat or even socks, I had to fight against frightful winter weather in Seoul. My feet were soon frozen through my rubber shoes, and the bone chilling cold was hard to bear. In a few minutes, I had lost all feeling in my body.

Fortunately, the House of Light, a group home for visually disabled, was located right next to the Seoul Train Station. I knew Evangelist Suk-Ahn Kim who resided there, but it was too early in the morning to pay him a visit. Of course, I knew that he would welcome me warmly and serve me a plate of hot breakfast while I warmed my body, but I didn't want to be a burden on him.

Instead, I waited in the lounge of the train station. Then I took the train that was headed to Hyo-Ja Dong. When I got off the train, lampposts, open sewers, and various carts in the street served as mischievous obstacles. The Seoul School for the Blind was on vacation. The outdoor gym had snow which came up to my knees and all the classrooms were empty. When I visited the dormitory, I was lucky enough to find two upperclassmen there. They led me to a warm room, and offered me a bowl of radish soup with rice along with icy kimchi that quenched my burning hunger instantly. It was a feast I will never forget for the rest of my life.

With the guidance of a friend, I entered into a dormitory room of my own. One dorm room had to be shared by five students. From the room, we walked about 300 meters to a well outside the dormitory. The water we filled up in a disfigured tin bucket was to be heated up and used to wash our face. The blind students would often trip and fall with the full bucket of water, enduring the subsequent pain which came from being engulfed in freezing water.

Although I didn't think this was the right place for me either, I ate for free because of my friends' generosity. Once I got friendly with the upperclassmen, I asked them how I might be able to enroll and study there. All of them agreed I would have to meet with teacher Soon-Hwa

Choi, the chairperson of the School for the Blind Committee in the district of Seoul. Encouraged by my supportive friends, I bought some dried persimmons and a bag of eggs with the little money I had earned from giving massages, and set out to pay him a visit.

After a big bow, I explained to him my desire to study at the Seoul School for the Blind. He told me that I should stay if I wanted to become a leader in the community, and commended me for my passion to further my education. But he also told me that the Seoul School for the Blind did not offer any scholarships, and therefore, I would have to pay for my own tuition and room and board. He asked me if I could come up with the money.

I told him that since I was part of the Light House Children's Society, they would sponsor me. He replied that my enrollment would depend on the outcome of the entrance exam. I raced back to Pusan in sheer ecstasy. I sought out my very best friend, Suk-Kwon Park, and asked him to run away with me to Seoul and study there together. Finally, February brought the first graduation of the Pusan School for the Blind. Immediately after graduation that night, we stole away to the Pusan Train Station and boarded a train to Seoul. It was only then I started to worry about the ticket master who constantly went up and down the aisle in search of people like us. I couldn't think of any way to slyly get past him. Then I noticed a policeman with his wife sitting across from us. I don't know what prompted me to tell them our situation, but when I did, they graciously made us part of their company so that the ticket master would not be suspicious of us.

As soon as we arrived at the Seoul Train Station, the policeman and his wife took us to a motel across from the station. As payment for getting us safely to Seoul, we felt compelled to give them our best massages.

When we arrived at the Seoul School for the Blind, the first and second testing periods were already over. Without filling out an application, we headed for the principal's office. The principal allowed us to start taking the test from the next period. The school was only accepting 15 students that year but had 35 applicants. However, we were proudly accepted into the school.

But the joy of acceptance lasted only for a precious while. We soon had to worry about presenting proof of graduation from our old school, as well as coming up with the registration fee and tuition. We had no choice but to return to Pusan and tell the truth to the head of our former school. He severely punished us and gave us a long lecture on how we had acted irresponsibly, but my friend Suk-Kwon was set on justifying our actions to him, and in the end, he granted us permission to attend the school in Seoul. Suk-Kwon and I returned safely back to Seoul with proof of graduation and we started our studies on the wooden floor of the Seoul School for the Blind.

Using the Wooden Floor as a Desk

Because we couldn't pay the registration fees, they were unable to assign us a desk for a month. We had to sit on the floor during every class period to receive our lessons. One afternoon, we had to endure humiliation from our homeroom teacher for not having paid our fees.

We had such a long way to go. Although we were willing to risk anything for a promise of a better education, not everything went as we had planned. I had no choice but to cling to God in prayer. I concluded that I could no longer survive in this place. "Lord, please move me to a school with a better environment. I can't stand the unfair treatment of the upperclassmen and neither can I stand the humiliation I have to endure everyday. Not only that, it is hard to just forget about all the times I was beaten and harassed for no apparent reason. Please God, save me from this place." I prayed in tears through the night under a big gingko tree.

One day, the school went on an outing to the outskirts of Chung-Nang City. The next day, everyone came down with typhoid fever—that is, everyone but me. The students were hospitalized in Sun-Hwa Hospital and the school temporarily canceled all classes.

With free time on my hands, I visited Elder Suk-Ahn Kim and explained to him my horrible situation. He told me that he had good news for me and gave me a recommendation to pass onto American Missionary Allen Clark. I traveled to the mission compound located on the 5th Street of Jongro. Reverend Clark, whose Korean name is Ahn-Jun Kwak, was the president of Pyongyang Seminary who happened to be in search of a young blind student to sponsor. We came to an agreement that day that he would pay for my tuition under the condition that I studied the Bible with him.

A Blind Student in a Regular High School

I took my meeting with Reverend Clark as an answer to my prayers, and gave a notice of voluntary withdrawal from Seoul School for the Blind. When I received the report card, I had achieved high marks in every class except for the Massage Class.

For several months, I attended a learning center to prepare myself for the entrance exam and studied the Bible just as I had promised Reverend Clark. Early one spring morning, guided by Elder Suk-Ahn Kim, I entered the doors of Soongsil High School with ambitious dreams in order to take the entrance exam. Three people gave me a warm welcome: Principal Chi-Sung Kim, Elder Koo-Jun Kim and Teacher Bong-Jun Lee. After talking to Principal Kim, he asked me. "We only have regular students. How do you expect to study here as a blind student? How about we take the test first and see."

"Do as you please. I will try my best," I replied.

So I started to take the test with a typewriter I had learned to use. The entrance exam took a very long time. Because most of the problems were ones I had already studied at the learning center, I was able to pass without much difficulty. I was admitted as a freshman to the prestigious Soongsil High School, renowned for its history and tradition.

Although I didn't have a single family member to share my joy with, I thanked the Holy Spirit and gave glory to God. Despite my blindness, the fact that I could have three thousand non-handicapped fellow students became another milestone in my life.

Not only did I do my best in all the regular classes I took, but I never lost my smile as I endured any difficulty with a healthy frame of mind. Because they didn't even have Braille textbooks, it was close to impossible to catch up to the rest of the class. Needless to say, I couldn't have finished high school without the sacrificial help of my friends. I took notes by making Braille letters as my friends whispered what had been written on the blackboard. After school, they read the textbook to me, and I made a Braille translation of the text. Many times, my fingers were severely bruised, but I did my best.

I memorized English vocabulary and solved math problems until midnight with my friends. I went to the Freedom Church for early morning service at 5 o'clock every morning and would directly go to my classes afterwards. I ate a piece of bread for breakfast. Without being diligent and faithful, it was impossible to survive in the regular school as the only blind student. Thinking back, it seems I had spent some miraculous days there.

Besides my studies, I remember the tight bond of love created between the teachers and students through the warm and valuable teachings they provided for us. Although there were countless teachers who loved and cared for us, Teacher Jung-Doo Lee who is still alive to this day, and Teacher Sung-Yup Lee who now lives in America, stand out in my memory as two teachers who provided me with such tender loving care.

I participated in all the events as an equal to my classmates with much confidence. Having a handicap did not prevent me from fulfilling my duties and treating the lower classmen with loving care. Before long, my friends offered to carry my backpack from the bus stop to school. We would walk to school together arm-in-arm, and they helped me in school to attend classes without much difficulty. There was even a saying going around that whoever bothered Sun-Tae would pay for it. I was able to safely finish my studies in such a supportive and protective environment. Just as I was the respected king of beggars, I spent my dream-filled high school years as the king of the students.

The Miracle After
the Thirty-Third Try

The Opportunity of College Admission Offered to the Blind

In the first semester of my last year at Soongsil High School, the infamous military revolution took place on a May 16th. In that turmoil, I graduated from high school, becoming the first visually disabled person to graduate from my school. However, the military revolution proved to be a great obstacle in my attempt to enter college.

The military government had reformed the educational system as a result of the social revolution. In order to enter college, you had to pass the college entrance exam given by the government. The test was divided into two parts: a written portion worth 250 points, and the physical test worth 50 points. When I had filled out the application and sent it in to take the test, I was given a rejection notice. Under the reformed educational system, those with disabilities were no longer allowed to enter college. Now that the military had taken over the government, there was not a soul in the country who could possibly oppose them.

I couldn't do anything but despair. But a ray of hope penetrated through my heart. Did I not succeed in escaping from the valley of death and despair? Having decided that nothing in the world could block my path, I decided to embark on a new adventure that would lead me to another door of success.

The next day, as soon as I arrived at school, I visited the principal's office.

"Please open the door to my college admission," I said firmly.

"Didn't you already get a rejection notice from the Department of Education?"

"If you will only leave everything to me, I will take care of it," I replied adamantly.

"How in the world will you take care of this problem?" He asked me rather curiously.

"Leave the strategy up to me. I will surely succeed."

"Wow! You are more stubborn than I thought. Okay, you try it your way." He finally gave in.

Although I had the school's permission to pursue further, I was worried to death. Later, I went in search of the Department of Education head, Mr. Choi.

"Please give blind students a chance to enter college as well," I said as soon as I met him.

"We just had a meeting regarding that issue with the Department. But right now, it is impossible with the current reformed law. The law must be changed in order for the handicapped to enter college." His reply was cold and unsympathetic.

"You people say the Republic of Korea is a democratic nation. But how is it practicing democracy when it will not allow blind people the freedom to pursue further education? You called for a revolution, but it's turning into a plain dictatorship." I declared excitedly. Mr. Choi didn't budge.

"Hey, it's not me that's not letting you go to college. It's the law of this country." He argued unabated.

"What kind of a nonsensical argument is that? For whom does the law exist? Is the law something that falls out of the clear blue sky? Aren't such laws made by people like you?" I wasn't going to give up. Not just yet. Not in million years.

"No matter what you say, it won't work. So don't waste your energy here. Go home."

"Fine, I'm going back today because I'm hungry. I'll be back tomorrow." And I left.

Cracking a Big Rock With an Egg

I went back the next day and stood before the same man.
"I'm back."

"Why you! Wasn't what I told you yesterday enough? Why are you back?" said Mr. Choi with agitation.

"I have fought a hard fight up to today in order to go to college. How can you tell me to give up so easily? Whatever you do, just open up a door for me to continue my education." I stood still in front of Mr. Choi with my feet firmly planted on the ground. Mr. Choi finally yelled at me.

"I'm busy, boy! Get out of here!"

In order to show him that even a blind student could learn, I started to recite English vocabulary aloud in front of his desk. I felt as if all the English textbooks from my first to last year in high school had been opened in my mind. I recited the English textbook aloud until I foamed at the mouth. I could feel the pitying stares of the workers in that office.

I went back to the same place the next day. As I entered the office of Mr. Choi, a worker joked, "Mr. Choi, here comes your long awaited guest."

I went up to Mr. Choi and took a deep bow. "I'm back."

This time, Mr. Choi completely ignored me. I went back every single day. The fourth day, the fifth day, the sixth day... I visited him a total of thirty-three times. But no matter how many times I went back, the chair of the department did not bend. I felt like I was hitting a rock with an egg. Having decided that this would never work, I resorted to my last strategy on the thirty-third day. I went back to Mr. Choi's office with a sharp knife hidden inside of my coat.

"Are you really refusing the request of a blind man?" I said.

"How many times do I have to tell you, you bastard! If I say 'no', it means 'no'!" He started pounding on the table with anger. I took out the knife I had been hiding.

"Mr. Choi, you are the kind of enemy that is making our country into a third world nation. It is a shame that a person like you is occupying the head chair in this country's Department of Education. You and I should die together so that a better person who will reform the education laws of this country will take over your position--a person who will grant the right to college education even to the blind." I ran in Mr. Choi's direction with the knife pointed directly at him.

"Meet your death!" I shouted.

Mr. Choi retreated. "Can you please put down that knife?" He spoke nervously.

"Why should I put away the knife? You and I should die together!" I shouted again.

I went after Mr. Choi like a madman. All the workers evacuated the room in a matter of seconds. What was happening soon spread to the news reporters who were in the building. All the reporters flocked together and encouraged me as they took pictures.

"You are right! It makes no sense that a so-called democratic country would deny blind people the right to pursue education. Hurray, Sun Tae Kim, hurray!" They cheered me on.

Nothing is Impossible

The next day in the Daily Korea Times, the article on Sun Tae Kim filled up the entire Community section of the newspaper. After my story had been published in the paper, many people recognized me. Sometimes in the bus, passengers whispered to each other, "He was in the papers." Some even came up to me and said, "I saw you in the paper. I wish you success," and encouraged me. The driver didn't even charge me bus fare. Not only that, the restaurant owners did not charge me after meals, and I was given free medicine when I went into drugstores. I had become an instant celebrity for several months.

As I became well known in the community, I even received letters from girls who wanted to date me. The head of the Educational Department sent a special order to the college authorities allowing the blind to take the college entrance exams. I had made the impossible possible after thirty-three tries. As a blind man, I was admitted into Soongsil University after overcoming many obstacles.

Although I had forced my way into taking the entrance exam, they were adamant against me taking the physical aptitude test which counted for 50 points. Another obstacle was blocking my path. I did not give up but agreed to take only the written test and trusted in God's help. As I had expected, I did not receive any score for the physical aptitude section. My university entrance score was to be comprised solely of my written test score.

The Day I Entered Soongsil University

God gave me wisdom. I decided to submit my application to Soongsil University where they understood my situation. Soongsil's foundation was built upon godliness. I was finally admitted to a university—the place I had sought all my life. When I received the acceptance letter, tears drenched my cheeks. But I had no mother or father, sister or brother to share my joy with. I took the acceptance letter to the Han River. Although I couldn't see the river, I drew the Han River in my mind as I stared into the water with tears streaming down my face. I was constructing my future before my eyes. Despite the cold weather, I stayed there for two hours, and I returned to my place in the twilight.

Even though I was admitted to the school, the dorm supervisor told me that they could not provide me with a room. With the help of a former superintendent of the school, I was granted a room which four students shared two separate bunk beds. Including myself, all four of us who shared the room became full-time ministers in later years. The oldest one among us became a missionary to Indonesia. We prayed together day and night, and we kept a strict balance between our school studies and spiritual discipline. Soongsil's ideal environment for academic pursuit and ministerial activities became the important underlying factor in integrating my intelligence and faith throughout my twenties.

My Motive in Studying Philosophy

What Philosophy Means to Me

I had a motive for choosing philosophy as my major at Soongsil University. In order to become a great pastor and minister for the blind, I needed a shortcut to hone my skills. I heeded the advice of some pastors I had always respected and decided to enter as a philosophy major.

Philosophy means "love of wisdom and knowledge." The meaning is derived from the Hellenistic mindset that promotes fostering knowledge through the pursuit of scholarly endeavors. How can one become a mentor without having cultivated a scholarly intellect? I had concluded that without the basic knowledge of the thoughts procured by many philosophers of the past, I would never be able to understand the study of God. And so to truly understand "theology", I challenged myself with such a grand and difficult major as philosophy.

Although Soongsil was a Christian college, the Philosophy Department was by no means obscured by the narrow field of Christian philosophy. I studied the basic courses in philosophy with diligence. Sometimes, the pedantic aspects of philosophy proved difficult, but I did my best to use reason in all of my thinking faculties as well as in my judgment and analysis.

Whenever I encountered a philosophical idea or a thought, I was able to discover the main drift of public opinion which formed that particular thought during that particular period. I also reached the point where I attempted to establish and clarify a basis for my own ideas and way of approaching philosophy. However, I never lost sight of the fact that philosophy was simply a supplementary discipline I was training myself in for the sake of future ministry to the unfortunate, suffering people like myself. I realized that my philosophical methodology, position, and scope first had to be firmly in place in order for my behavioral philosophy to be strongly rooted and shaped through the discipline of theology.

Not only did I pursue philosophy as a basis for my future theological training, but I also focused on studying sociology and psychology as a means to broaden my understanding in every scholarly field through depth and breadth. Such scholarly attitudes assisted me greatly later in life as I received my theological training.

Had I not faithfully laid the foundation for my theological studies, I would have faced many doubts and failures during my later years of obtaining a Masters in Divinity and Ph.D. While I was studying the philosophy of ministry at McCormick Seminary in Chicago, my philosophical training paid off as I realized that theories and utilization thereof can only be made possible through the synthesis of intellectual methodologies and practical applications.

For the advancement of my education, I realized I had to master English as well as other foreign languages. Especially for me to continue my scholarly endeavors within the American education system, I knew the importance of acquiring a high level of fluency in my conversational English. Therefore, I did my best to become competent in English and other foreign languages.

The four years I spent at Soongsil, my sanctuary of learning, was hardly enough to satisfy a twenty-some year old intellectual like myself with so many unfulfilled dreams. I felt like if I didn't somehow divide my 24 hours into 48, I wouldn't even be able to pass any of my classes. This thought kept me running in every possible way, pursuing a glimpse of success and excellence which I knew would be mine one day.

Studying, however, wasn't the only thing I needed to become competent to enroll in seminary. I counted spiritual discipline and sacrificial service to be of greater value in my pursuit of holiness. Without the practice of strict spiritual discipline, I realized the life of a minister could become very superficial. Because ministry can easily turn into a business, I was careful to draw boundaries early in my studies.

My Role Model, Teacher Chang-Ho Ahn

During my years at Soongsil University, I invested my time and interest into building up godly character. I constantly kept myself accountable through repentance and prayer, without neglecting the discipline of meditation that allowed me to communicate with the spiritual world. More than anything, I valued fostering the image of Christ through a life of self-denial and sacrificial service.

In my endless attempt to attain deep spiritual form, Teacher Chang-Ho Ahn, who completely gave himself up for the respect and independence of his country, moved me deeply and became my role model.

I went to Freedom Church every Sunday and taught Sunday school to the junior and senior high school students. The church was located on a hill that was a 40-minute walk. Although there were many obstacles on the road, I safely navigated around them with the help of students who were also on their way to church.

Since everyone was poor at the time, the only thing we could afford to share with each other at the youth meeting was a cheap, stale loaf of bread. The church finances did not allow the church to buy even a bowl of noodles for the teachers.

The Life of Poverty:
A Required Course in the Field of Spiritual Discipline

For me a life of poverty was an absolute necessity in building up virtue as well as a good training exercise in spiritual discipline. Serving at a church that couldn't even offer me bus fare provided me with precious training experience.

I decided to cut down on my meal tickets. Fasting for the sake of other necessary tasks, I skipped one meal a day for an indefinite period. Sometimes, I would fast two meals a day, and other times, I would go on for two or three days solely on water so that I might share in the fellowship of His sufferings. I was adjusting to fasting and prayer without physical illness.

Fasting was also a necessary discipline in shedding greed and vanity. The money I had saved from my meal tickets was used for offerings, transportation fees, laundry and other living expenses. With any left over money, I bought snacks to share with the students I was teaching.

I discovered another spiritual discipline I was able to take delight in while serving the church. I reasoned that if I were to cut down on the transportation cost to and from church, I would be able to help those people in a worse situation than myself. I decided to carry out this plan.

I also visited an orphanage twice a month where uninfected children of lepers were housed. With a hundred inhabitants, they desperately needed help. It was a perfect place to offer my services.

I tutored them, read them fairy tales, sang children's gospel songs and ran around with them. Sometimes, I brought silkworm pupas and popcorn to share with them. They would swing from my arms as they pleaded with me to stay and live with them. For a year and a half, my friend In-Suh Lee and I served together as we practiced a life of poverty.

Tuition Goes as an Offering for the Building of a New Church

Through the introduction of my friend, Sang-Wook Lee, I was given yet another chance to dedicate myself to God's service. I believe this opportunity was the most difficult and required my complete sacrifice and service out of all the spiritual disciplines God was teaching me in my fourth year in college. It not only required a physical sacrifice, but the sacrifice of all entire material possessions.

"Sun Tae, you are good at teaching Sunday school. How would you like to help out with the newly started church I serve at?"

Through my friend's urging, I started attending a newly established church for the first time in my life. There was more than enough work to be done. From teaching the little kids to directing the choir, my life of service demanded complete sacrifice.

After several weeks, we were asked to start a Vacation Bible School with a budget of zero. I asked for funds from the elders I had known from elsewhere, and I was able to collect a handsome amount of offerings—

enough to buy books and snacks to proceed with the Vacation Bible Shool.

The day after the Vacation Bible School was over, I received news from Sang Wook that the city had demolished the church building because it did not have a license. At the time, finishing up my graduation was taking up all my time and energy. And being only a poor college student, I had no way of helping the church.

To tell the truth, I was able to stay in the dorm as a special favor from the dorm supervisor, Elder Lee. I attempted to pay back the favor by massaging Elder Lee's paralyzed wife with much devotion. Elder Lee treated me like his son, and he would even lend me money in cases of emergency.

As I prayed together with the congregation at the demolished building site, I thought about what I could do to help. But not having any money, there was no way for me to give an offering. The only money I had was my next semester's tuition and money for my room and board.

Except for the room and board expenses, I gave all my tuition money as an offering to the church. We prayed for a place where we could build a place of worship. Thinking back on it now, I wonder if that wasn't the basis of my learning the spiritual discipline of dedication and service.

Without having completed my registration process, I entered into my last semester of college. I received a letter from the office of Treasury, and the school urging me daily to pay my tuition. I had no choice but to sell my invaluable used books to the lower classmen, hoping to raise 15,500 won, but was only able to raise half that amount.

The Dean of the Students called me into his office and scolded me for not having paid the tuition. He accused me of having the mindset of a thief and threatened to expel me if I did not pay my tuition soon.

I was crushed. But I didn't tell him that I had given my tuition away as an offering; I didn't try to make him understand. I told him that I would keep my promise if he would just give me a couple of more days. He consented because he said that I had always been faithful to my word. I needed to somehow come up with the money in a hurry.

I grabbed my flute and started wandering around in rich neighborhoods. Imagine the scene. A masseur would usually wear a suit with a tie. I had neither. It was understandable to be rejected because I was in casual school clothes. For five days, I continued and prayed, "God, please help me."

A Cup of Hot Chocolate and a Baked Sweet Potato

On Friday night as I played the melodious tune on my flute, an aged man invited me into his second floor flat. Seeing my school badge, he asked me if I was a student. He offered me some hot chocolate and a baked sweet potato.

After being served, I washed my hands and began to massage him with care. We shared our life stories together. He told me all about himself. The elderly man was a fervent Christian who had fled from the

North. As a refugee, he lived near Soongsil University.

He asked me how much I needed for tuition. He not only gave me enough money for tuition, but also an additional 2,000 won for personal use. Although he had lived a life of poverty and was poor even now, making a living selling vegetables, he told me to accept his gift because I seemed to be in a dire situation. He urged me to be a person of great stature and honor before God. He chose to remain anonymous until the end. Because of his kind care and love, I was able to pay off my tuition and had enough to give an offering of thanksgiving to my church.

As you have read above, my college life was necessary training for me to build up my spiritual discipline to study theology in the years to come.

A few years ago, I had the opportunity to visit Shin Kwang Church where I gave up my tuition as an offering for the building. I witnessed how it has developed into a beautiful church in the heart of Bongchung. I met some of my ex-students who have become successful business people and leaders of the church. Among them, one had become the head official of Korean Air and another was running a large business in New Zealand.

Spiritual Discipline and Theology

Entrance to Seminary

It took me twenty-some years of prayer and preparation to enter seminary. Having entered seminary at twenty-six, the three years I had spent there could well be included in the golden years of my twenties. Seminary studies could not be delayed anymore for a person who had dedicated himself to prepare for the Lord's ministry. After the graduation exam at the university, I could no longer reside in the dormitory. While deciding where to stay, I asked one of the upperclassmen for help. He had purchased a thousand *pyung* of land (approximately 4,000 square yards) and built a two-room shack. He rented out one room and offered to let me live with him in the other room. He only required me to pay for food and suggested that I live there until I enrolled in seminary.

Sharing a room was uncomfortable, however because, he constantly borrowed money from me to pay off his application fees for graduate school, transportation costs and other living expenses without the least intention of paying me back. In a short while, I too was broke. I had to borrow money from friends to apply to seminary. After doing well on the entrance exam and having a good interview, I received an acceptance notice in the mail.

Miracles Happen Through God's People

A year before I entered seminary, I happened to run into Professor Sun-Ae Joo who had transferred from Soongsil University to the Presbyterian Theological Seminary as a Professor of Theology. When I met him on the campus of Soongsil University, he congratulated me on my acceptance to the school. I was overjoyed. But I did not have the 13,000 won I needed for the first year tuition. I went to the hills behind Soongsil University where they had erected a wooden cross. Embracing the cross, I cried and prayed aloud. After a while, I looked around hoping a miracle might have happened. Nothing. But miracles often come through God's people. After the prayer, as I walked past the chaplain's office, I ran into Reverend Eun-Soo Oh. With one glance at my face, he asked if something was wrong. I told him my story.

He invited me to the chaplain's office and made a call to Missionary Harold Voelkel whose Korean name was Ho-Yul Ok, telling him my situation. Hanging up the phone, he urged me to go to the Department of

Missions immediately. I ran. Reverend Voelkel and his wife greeted me warmly, and listened to all my problems patiently. The day was extremely cold and it was snowing outside. A hot cup of black tea with a couple of biscuits helped thaw my body. Just imagine my joy at having received an answer to my prayer so soon. Reverend Voelkel handed me an envelope with my tuition. With tears of gratitude streaming down my face, I didn't lose a minute in catching the bus to the Presbyterian Seminary on that cold Saturday afternoon. However, when I got there, they had already closed down for the day. I had to wait until Monday, which was the last day of registration.

Battling with the Entrance Measles All Over Again

I wanted to check my name on the registration roster just to be sure. I was in for another surprise; my name was under the list of auditors. Shocked, I immediately called Professor Sun-Ae Joo and Professor Jong-Sung Lee. Professor Lee told me that all admitted students had to get his approval, and that there must have been some administrative error.

I had to battle with the entrance measles all over again. Why is it that I always had to jump over so many obstacles whenever I was faced with a new situation? If I had really been admitted with a top score, why did I have to enter as an auditing student? And if I had no choice but to enter seminary as an auditor, I wondered if it was really worth the effort. I wanted to clear up the issue more than ever.

When I returned on Monday morning to pay my tuition, I met Professor Chang-Hwan Park who left a very good impression on me. Professor Park explained to me that there was another blind student who had enrolled the year before. He was not able to carry out the class load and faced many difficulties. After the seminary's experience with him, Professor Park thought it best to offer me an auditor's enrollment for a year, and they would observe my progress. He apologized that he had not known I had graduated from a regular middle school, high school, and college, and allowed me to enroll in a three-year program with all fairness.

After that incident, Professor Park spent the next five years alongside me as my teacher and mentor while I finished my Masters degree. From the mid 1980's, whenever I have a chance to visit Korean immigrant churches in America, I try to meet with Professor Park to share some old memories together and renew our mentor-disciple relationship.

There were too many courses to be completed during three years of seminary. New Testament Theology, Old Testament Theology, Systematic Theology, Practical Theology, Pastoral Studies, the list was endless. One had to earn 120 credit hours in order to graduate. Not only that, Greek and Hebrew had to be taken all three years. I had never imagined theological studies to be so demanding. Compared to my college years, the three-year program was much more challenging because of specialized area of studies. Without having any time to spend in fellowship with other students, I had to race through my seminary years.

I believe there were a total of 40 students enrolled that year. They came from all different colleges. Some came with recommendations from the presbytery; but all came with the vision of preparing for a future ministry. A tremendous age gap existed between students. I even found myself studying with an evangelist in his early 40's.

It didn't seem as though all of them came to major in ministry, however. There were some who came with a burning sense of calling, only to quit after a semester of studies because they didn't think they could accomplish what they had come to do. Other students still had a college mentality of only pursuing academic success. Therefore, they would get top grades even at the cost of neglecting their prayer life and spiritual disciplines. Professors went to great lengths to explain that seminary wasn't a place to simply satisfy academic pursuits, nor a place to produce intellectuals, but a place to train tomorrow's leaders to lead the people into God's kingdom with a strong sense of calling. Every professor emphasized the importance of forming godly character and practicing spiritual disciplines.

Every day at the seminary was like carrying a huge wooden cross on my back. First, it was difficult for me to understand and be on track with all my classes. In addition, I was having spiritual struggles which added weight to the cross I was carrying. Although I tried to obey Jesus' teaching to "deny yourself and pick up your cross daily, and follow me," there constantly appeared before me situations I had no control over, like a gigantic mountain that made it difficult for me to take a single step forward.

In Between Pastoral Ministry and Theology

As the end of the first semester drew near, I let out a sigh of relief. As I heard the stories of God's world and the history of the church, my spirit was revived like it had drunk gulps of spring water. An amazing confession of faith regarding God's providence and guidance of the Holy Spirit arose out of the ashes of despair.

Including myself, every individual in my class had their own unique characteristics. I was able to discover the importance of fellowship through this realization. Because of the differences in their approach to theology, there was a natural division in the field of ministry. For example, there was the scholastic theologian group and the church growth analysts. Those especially interested in becoming revival guest speakers developed their own unique style of preaching. I clearly recognized how pastoral ministry and theology complemented each other. But integrating the two took time. I spent the next twenty years pastoring as I explored the integral relationship that existed between the two. In doing so, I was able to construct a comprehensive theology of pastoral ministry. The students interested in becoming seminary professors influenced my theological spiritual formation, and the group of revivalist students influenced my practical spiritual formation. Such influences were central in balancing my theology.

The spring of 1966 was extremely warm. About 500 students were enrolled in the main Divinity Program, adjunct seminary studies or the

Department of Christian Education. There was only a meager staff of seven professors. From time to time, renowned theology professors from the US Presbytery or the Presbytery of Korea came to lecture as visiting professors. They were all so proficient in Korean and in delivering excellent lectures.

Living a Life Without
Material Possessions

Spiritual Discipline Through Frugality and Poverty

I was able to pay for my tuition, room and board, and transportation fees through the mission support I had received throughout my seminary studies. Because it was never enough, I had to rely on individual charitable sources. The involuntary fasting that came with the life of frugality and poverty was indeed difficult spiritual training to endure. Many times, I walked deep into the woods and felt God's true existence and the Holy Spirit's presence as I held unto the pine trees and prayed.

The degree of spiritual discipline and character formation needed to produce a prophet was tremendous. It was similar to how Daniel and his friends had to refuse the court's rich meat and wine and live on only vegetables and water. Not only that, they had to face the lion in the lion's den, undergoing near-death experiences which refined their spirits as if in a furnace.

Whenever summer or winter vacation rolled around, everyone returned home. Some would come back in new clothes or bring tasty side dishes. Some friends even got married at that time. But I always had to wear the same clothes and go without clean undergarments. Like a monk in a monastery, I had no choice but to devote myself to poverty and starvation. With my every turn, Jesus was there at my side comforting me with these words: "I am sharing in your sufferings".

Training in frugality and poverty involved some practical problems. The first thing I had to control was my appetite. Not having enough money to eat three meals a day, I had to fast lunch as I had done through-out in college. During that hour, I meditated on Christ as I took long walks. Sometimes, I went to the organ room and spent my time in praise and worship playing hymns.

There was even a time I had to use disposable wooden chopsticks for a whole month. They decayed and turned black that I had no choice but to throw them away. Out of the numerous people in the world, I believed it was my special calling to undergo much suffering in order that I might find my true identity. I viewed these hardships as spiritual training to become a chosen servant of God. Therefore, even in small matters, I had complete determination because I believed developing complete self-control was a necessary virtue in my training.

Living for two years with only one set of clothes also contributed to my life of absolute frugality which monks consider their calling. Some days, continuous cold weather did not give me a chance to wash the only undergarment I had. On those days, being self-conscious, I made an effort to keep at an extra distance from my classmates though I tried not to show it.

The seminary cafeteria used a system operated by meal tickets. A meal cost 13 won, but the food was just horrible. I was malnourished to the point of fainting, but I did not falter from my belief that spiritual power and character was developed only through a life of complete self-control. Although I did not consider myself to practice strict asceticism, I believed I had to restrain one's passion for food. From time to time, I would imagine the greatest feast unfolding before my eyes. But how could I beg God for food like a little child?

Because I did not have a cotton-stuffed blanket for winter, I had to wrap two thin blankets together to cover myself. I shuddered throughout the night as the chilly draft swept over me from head to toe, constantly disturbing my slumber. Imagine sleeping in a climate 10-15 degrees below zero in a room where the furnace often went out on you. Imagine lying on the cold concrete floor with the cold air seeping through the thin and shabby window frames. I assure you that the experience makes you feel as though your body has turned itself into a big human icicle. I would often remember dreaming about my childhood years when I used to sleep inside a warm and cozy cotton blanket.

Through such a life of frugality and poverty, I constructed my glorious future. Just like the Shalom Covenant God had entered into with Noah, I drew up many contracts between God and myself regarding the management of my future assets. I made sure I had set apart the first fruits of my earning as an offering to God along with the offering of my service. I had decided that as I had given the first fruits from my years as a beggar, I should be a good steward with any profit which came into my hands.

Answer to a Prayer Offered up During Hard Times

Several part-time jobs were offered to seminarians. Once I had heard that an evening Bible Study group was looking for an English teacher. I went for an interview. Unfortunately, I was rejected because of my blindness. With deep frustration, I prayed to God defiantly, "Even if you had at least preserved one of my eyes, I would not have missed this opportunity!"

However, I did not forget that even a prayer offered in defiance would someday reap fruit. Through many occasions, I was getting used to calming my temper down by wiping my tears, as if I had predisposition to do so. The verse from John I had read as a little child comforted me greatly.

"And I will do whatever you ask in my name, so that the Son may bring glory to the Father. You may ask me for anything in my name, and I will do it." (John 14:13-14)

"If you remain in me and my words remain in you, ask whatever you wish, and it will be given you." (John 15:7).

God Who Provides

One day, Reverend Do who cared greatly for my well-being, called for me. He had been suffering from arthritis for a long time. He asked, "Sun Tae, do you know how to give a massage?"

"Yes, I know, Professor," I replied.

He requested I come to his house twice a week to give him a massage. I chose Mondays and Saturdays when I had no classes. Although I had no formal training, I did my best. As a result, his pain lessened considerably. Usually after the massage session, his wife set a full table before me and asked me to eat. The abundant amounts of white rice, bean paste soup, and well fermented *kimchi* were more delicious than any delicacies I could imagine.

As the summer vacation drew near, I was worried about raising money for my tuition. Just then, the chair of Practical Theology, Professor Kyu-Dang Kim, asked to meet with me. He told me that if I served at any place during the summer, he would provide me with fall tuition. It was truly wonderful news. I immediately met with an upperclassman who worked at an orphanage about twenty minutes away from the seminary. He agreed wholeheartedly and told me to come anytime to serve at his orphanage.

With my friend's permission, I became a counselor and teacher to the orphans. Every evening I taught them the Bible and we sang praises together. Sometimes, I even acted out Bible stories. In such ways, I soon felt like I was becoming a part of the family. For two months, sleeping and eating with them at the orphanage, I had no worries about room and board. The students grew very fond of me to such a degree that I would receive love letters from eligible young ladies at the orphanage.

With the pay I received at the end of two months, I was able to pay my tuition. Did not the Apostle Paul consider all things rubbish compared to knowing Christ? In the same way, I realized that unless I considered money and honor as rubbish in the journey of becoming God's chosen servant, dedication and sacrifice were simply impossible.

What I Realized by Serving Without Compensation

Every seminarian must choose either a Children, Youth, College, or Young Adult group to serve to receive credit for their field education requirement. Conveniently, a pastor I had known for a while invited me to come serve at the church where he had just been transferred to. At his request I started teaching the elementary, junior and senior high school students there. Initially, there were only forty elementary students and about twenty junior and senior high school students. In less than a month, the elementary members increased to a hundred and the youth group grew to sixty students.

Despite my two months of service, I was unable to receive any sort of compensation or transportation costs. I wasn't complaining that I had to serve while emptying my own pockets. Even if my friend wanted to give me some compensation, the church finances had hit rock bottom. More than that, the lack of interest from the church board shattered my heart to pieces.

One Saturday afternoon, after the Youth Program, I had to return to the seminary. But to my dismay, I didn't have a single bus ticket in my possession. The way back was so long, I had to transfer buses. I couldn't think of anything better than to get on the bus and plead for the driver's mercy. The driver was indeed gracious when I explained my situation.

I got off at my stop. Although I had to cross the street and transfer to another bus, my pride did not allow me to beg for a second time. I decided to walk from there to the seminary. When I arrived at school with brisk steps to make it there before the national curfew, the school gates were firmly locked. Not wanting to disturb my friends' peaceful slumber, I roamed about the school premises until I ran into the security guard, Elder Hong. I politely asked him to open the sanctuary for me. Shivering in the cold sanctuary, I prayed until dawn and returned to my room shortly after. My roommate, Chun-Kyu Im, told me he was worried something had happened to me on the way back from the church and had a very restless night waiting for me. Overcoming such difficulties, I served at that church for a year and a half.

After offering a year and a half of free service to the church, I felt the emptiness that came with my resignation. Although people may love money and attempt to serve both God and riches, it is impossible for those who are called to His ministry to lead such self-centered lives. We must throw away our wrong attitudes about our job and our greed for money. Tired and worn out, I waited for God's guidance for another opportunity to serve.

It was in those days brother Hwang, who is currently pastoring a church in Jacksonville, Florida, came to me with good news. The Mirim Lumber Company was willing to give me a scholarship for the remainder of my two semesters. It was quite a heavenly bit of news. One and a half years of accumulated weariness was lifted off my shoulders that instant.

I had thought that asking those who have shared in the Lord's ministry to serve without any compensation was a harsh request. That experience had taught me an invaluable lesson I preciously retained during my latter ministry years.

I sought out a place that required my love and started serving at the Emmanuel Blind Women's Group Home in the district of Dobong. They welcomed me as warmly as they would a real brother. I deeply felt that I needed to go to a place where they desperately needed me. Although the places I had to tend to were like rocky paths and the fields of thorns, I realized I must receive my mission with the heart of a farmer who turns those places into good soil in order to sow the seeds of the gospel.

I often prayed, "Lord, as I adore you, please give me the strength to love all the people who are in need of me. Please give me insight so that I might not become a shortsighted leader, that I may not become a blind man leading the blind to fall into the pit."

My Unforgettable
Seminarian Friends

Failed Plans

I thank God for the friends He had blessed me with during my seminary years, with whom I was able to share my future ministry dreams and
hopes. One day, brother Chang-Bok Chung, currently serving as a professor of Jangshin University, encountered the tragedy of losing his mother.
We all visited him and held a service at his place as well as contributed to
the funeral expenses. There is an episode behind the story of me giving
300 *won* which was quite a sum of money at that time for his mother's
funeral expenses.

On a cold winter afternoon, I had visited Reverend Samuel Moffet
who was a missionary. I explained to him my situation and towards the
evening, I received 500 *won* for my living expenses. As I was standing in
front of the store across from the school to buy daily necessities and food,
I ran into brother Hyung- Kil Kang who told me that he was collecting

money for the funeral expenses of brother Chang-Bok's mother. I had meant to give out only 200 *won* but by mistake I gave 300. I was too embarrassed to ask for 100 *won* in change so I simply had to settle for 200 *won* to purchase my personal needs. It seems like yesterday we were over at Chong Bok's house, comforting him as we stayed up for two nights eating red bean porridge together. Thirty years have already passed since then.

I believe I have been born with the blessing of meeting good people. I was able to meet a countless number of upper and lower classmen, fellow pastors, and thousands of brothers and sisters in the body of Christ. Among them, a friend cast a great vision for my life. Dr. Hyung-Kil Kang , currently pastoring at True Way Church in Chicago, gave me hope to study abroad in America.

Although my situation did not allow me to dream such dreams, I began six months of intensive studying for the TOEFL with his exhortation. He even wrote and mailed applications on my behalf to over twenty seminaries in America. Of those, I received an acceptance notice from about half. After I had taken the TOEFL, I applied for a scholarship at ten of those schools. But I was denied. My friend left for America alone as soon as he finished the graduation exams. I felt so empty and lonely coming back from the airport after seeing him off. My dream of becoming a professor in Korea after returning from studying and researching at a prominent American seminary had to remain as a wounded dream. I had to choose an alternative route to replace that dream.

I had made a firm decision to lead the life of a clergyman—a life devoid of any material possessions. In the New Testament, there are two types of people who serve the Lord: The first group is described as a select minority, leading a life devoid of material possessions like Jesus and the apostles; and the second group is categorized as using their wealth to help the evangelists and the church.

It would be impossible to live a clerical life devoid of material possessions unless one denies himself, picks up his cross, and follows Jesus with the attitude of a disciple. A shepherd must become a part of the minority and empty himself completely for the sake of gaining spiritual authority, capable of leading the flock on righteousness. All social groups in the world are designed to function and operate based on lineage or profit. However, we should never forget that spiritual groups established and rooted in Christ, function and operate upon the principal of the denial of material possessions.

As I listened to lectures on theology and pastoral ministry daily, ideas began to sink in. I was able to hear Jesus and the Holy Spirit's voice through the lectures delivered by my professors.

A Few Thoughts on the Philosophy of Ministry

Most of the students were required to get a recommendation from the Presbytery to serve at a church in order to complete their internship. These programs were supervised by the Professor of Practical Theology. I too had served at quite a few churches during my internship period. Sometimes, I would serve during Saturdays as well as instructing students at the church. I believed that 'a minister is to be the shepherd of the pasture', and so I actively attended every program and activity at the church. In order to discover my philosophy of ministry, I set up some rules and regulations.

First, I would not be church-centered but interact with a variety of churches. Secondly, I decided I would evaluate myself through constant self-examination regarding my leadership and through the conversations I held with classmates. Lastly, I would come to a definite decision of how I should present myself in my ministry. In other words, I wanted to be clear on the kind of image I would exude to others in my ministry.

Frankly speaking, maintenance of one's image is extremely important to a minister. One cannot be negligent when it comes to personal management. Because I was obsessed with the idea of overcoming my handicap, I had to be careful with every action.

Since character and dispositions are formed through shared emotions and building up of rapport between mutual relationships, I tried my best to interact with as many people as possible. I also made it a point to register their names and their activities of interest into my memory.

The environment at the seminary was always peaceful. The climax of the daily chapel service rested upon the spirit-filled praise time. For me, it was a time of refreshment when all my frustrations would melt away. Sometimes, they would hold revival meetings at school to encourage and emphasize the sense of calling for ministry. In those times, I experienced the burning desire and dedication to serve humbly and sacrificially. There were two in-school revival meetings. One was in the spring and the other in the fall. I was deeply moved after attending the revival meetings six consecutive times. The spectrum of speakers ranged widely from the conservative Presbyterians who emphasized the traditional view of Christianity, to the broad-minded liberals who emphasized pastoral ministry or the integration of holiness and academics. I also saw those who formed small groups to research further into their area of interest. As for me, I had no energy left to participate in such small groups. My days were already full with school studies and catching up with late assignments.

Rather than leaning toward the progressive and radical way of doing ministry, I found myself embracing the conservative view of moderateness in doing ministry. However, taking into consideration the unusual circumstances which my ministry pointed, I prayed fervently for the unique model of ministry I had in mind.

Are You Ready to Die For the Ministry to the Visually Disabled?

Since I had to cast a vision for 200,000 blind people, including myself, to secure an anchor of hope and light, I began to grope for a solution to the overwhelming project of a 'ministry to the blind' from many different angles. From surveying the present conditions of the blind to surveying the different social service organizations for the blind, I did not slack off for a moment. It was necessary for me to have the mentality of being a kernel of wheat that falls to the ground and dies for the sake of producing a seed of hope for the desperate blind people.

"Am I really ready to die for the ministry to the blind? Am I really preparing myself by storing within my body, mind and soul such latent energy of powerful vitality to become a kernel of wheat which will produce 30, 60, 100 times the result?" I could not help but constantly ask such questions. In order to reach my ideal, I had to first grow internally and keep a tight rein over the spirituality that can only arise from a life of poverty and humility, a life of complete denial of all earthly possessions.

Mere words never did the job. I had to show with actions and come up with programs that would persuade and attract the modern congregation toward a ministry for the blind. There were many times I would get depressed in the midst of asking questions to myself. In those times, I visited the chapel to meditate as I waited for His guidance.

Regardless of what form the ministry would take, I was adamant to make it one of strict volunteerism based on non-materialism. In order to do so, I reminded myself that my inner development and spiritual growth are of utmost importance in becoming an obedient kernel of grain. How could I possibly approach such ministry without having been spiritually clothed as the perfect bride of Christ like a pearl without any blemish?

My seminary years served as another period of spiritual discipline to construct my philosophy, target and direction of my ministry. I am grateful for the many things I was able to gain simply because of being enrolled in the seminary of the Presbyterian Church of Korea, which is the mother denomination for countless churches of great history and tradition.

As a matter of fact, I was an outsider to the ministry and an impossible case to be admitted into the field of theology. I cannot help but thank God who had granted me the opportunity to have various visions and bring them to fruition in such fertile soil, where faith, academics, and passion for missions were integrated into one, so that He might use me as His servant in ministry for the blind.

Not only that, I also thank God that I met many partners in ministry who could work with me as fellow missionaries and be shepherding co-workers even to this point in my life.

My Ideal Woman

If I Were to Marry

It was a period when I could not think about anything else because of the tremendous weight of my spiritual struggles and theological studies and activities. I felt rather detached from the approaching issue of marriage because I had dismissed it as an unattainable dream; a futile longing to be part of a painting on a wall.

But situations often undermine the logical mind, and opportunities arise like miracles. At the time, I felt that marriage was an unaffordable luxury for a seminarian without a house, money or even clothes to wear. However, women who wanted to marry me started to turn up one by one. I have no idea what they could have possibly seen in me. Since I was blind, I simply thought they were acting as helpful guides. I couldn't even imagine having any other feelings towards them.

One day, a member of a certain church asked me if I would be interested in going on an arranged date. I flatly refused. I told him that I had never even prayed about marriage, and, besides, I told him marriage definitely wasn't on my list of priorities. But the thought of an arranged date wasn't entirely unappealing.

Although I had a vague idea of my ideal woman I wished to marry, I didn't believe such a woman could easily be found. It was rather as if I had put up a guard. At least for me, marrying during my seminary years was forbidden. It was one of the limitations I had put on myself. For the first time in my life, I found myself in the chapel that night asking God about marriage as I fell into a deep meditation. I thought about the character and temperament of the woman I should marry.

My nervousness began to subside and an assurance rose within me. "If this is something You have allowed and are pleased with, I will obey." With that confession, I came out of the chapel.

Even under such difficult conditions, I fostered an innocent dream. 'How can I restore my lost family?' From time to time, as I reminisced about the happy childhood I spent with my parents, I would dream of having such a family of my own someday. Half of my classmates had already married and some even had several children. In a way, I was envious of them. I remember going to several of my friend's weddings. The holy matrimony being conducted with the blessings of many believers reminded me of the Wedding Feast of Cana which Jesus himself had blessed.

Who would be the bride that has been prepared for me at my once-in a-lifetime wedding feast? I started to imagine the detailed figure of my bride. My mother's youthful face came to my mind. With the beautiful smile and elegant features, she was the image of all mothers and my lasting image of an ideal woman. I wanted my other half, my life-long partner to possess much gentleness and kindness. Although I had lost my sight, I wished my partner to be without handicap. But I doubted an unimpaired woman would want to marry me.

Right before my seminary graduation, arranged dates kept rolling in. Since I had some confidence that I would become a pastor through my pastoral training and theological research, I accepted some of the requests. But it really was a dream come true when the woman who would become my partner in ministry appeared before my eyes one day.

It happened when my classmate Kwon-Sun Yoo suggested to set me up with a pretty lady with great faith. The three of us met at a ghetto Chinese restaurant on Ddook Island. My friend who was introducing us emphasized that the young lady came from a traditional Christian family and had great talent in music. One week later, Jung-Ja and I met alone. I explained my condition and situation to her in detail.

"I am a man devoid of any earthly possessions. I don't even have a house. Not only that, as you can see, I'm blind. But as a poor seminarian whose dreams and hopes are thrust upon the train of faith, I am sure of my future."

Her response to my self-introduction was brief and to the point, "If we lack money, we simply need to be frugal. We should use whatever God gives us with a thankful heart."

Then, I questioned her faith. "If you were forced by the communists under gunpoint, would you choose faith or communism?"

She answered without hesitation that she would choose faith. In other words, she was willing to be martyred. I was impressed. After several more meetings, we promised to be married. After praying, we decided to receive permission from her parents.

The Process of Receiving Permission to Marry

Jung-Ja's mother was against our marriage because I was blind, an orphan, and didn't even own a house. The reasons were obvious. The two of us did not despair but prayed while we waited for permission. Around that time, her mother needed a sudden operation due to an inflammation of the bladder. She was assigned to a hospital near the seminary where I was serving. During the surgery, she heard the voice of Jesus in her dream saying, "Do not oppose the marriage of your daughter to the blind intern pastor." That was the turning point. We received permission to be wed.

Two months later, in the middle of the fall semester of my second year in seminary, we held our engagement ceremony. Jung-Ja decided to marry me even after realizing my situation.

I asked her if she was ready to live with the people to whom I would be ministering. It was only after I received assurance in the form of her answer that we were engaged. Immediately after our engagement, she went to the live at the Immanuel House for the Blind Orphans located in Suyu-Ri. She thought in order to live with a blind husband, she needed training to understand him. She adapted well to the environment for the next two years.

Finally, we decided on a wedding date. It was to be November 23, 1968, a day I will never forget. But there awaited another catastrophe right before the wedding day.

The Miracle That Took Place a Day Before the Wedding

On the day before the wedding, I was in my dorm, studying for my finals and preparing my graduation thesis. Early on my wedding day, I went to chapel and attended the morning service. When I came back to my room, I turned on the radio. The broadcast reported a fire which had started at the South Gate Open Market and set the entire business district on fire–that was the very location where Jung-Ja lived. The situation indicated no survivors. However, I went to class and sat through a two-hour lecture, completely worry-free. Afterwards, my friends and I headed to Sung-Do Church where my wedding was to be held.

As long as God was alive and at work, I believed He would not allow my bride to perish in flames. Her family was a God-fearing family for generations. Her maternal grandfather was a great evangelist in Hwang-

Hae Island. I didn't believe God was going to bring tragedy upon such a family. Although I did believe in divine intervention, I couldn't help harboring some anxiety in the corner of my heart.

I carefully ironed the one and only suit I wore everyday, and went to church to wait for my bride. Guests began arriving one by one. I thought how humiliating it would be if the bride didn't show up with everyone waiting. I don't know how much time passed until the father and mother of the bride finally came through the door. As soon as they saw me, they offered up a prayer of thanksgiving as they told me how God had saved them.

The fire had started from a house in front of Jung-Ja's house. The entire district was burned to ashes except for a few houses, including Jung-Ja's. It was truly a miracle. When I visited her house a few days later, I could still feel the heat from scorched walls. They had escaped a very close call.

After our wedding ceremony, I told Jung-Ja, "You know, it's not very becoming of us to go to Cheju Island, Kyungju, Sooahn or Sorak Mountain for our honeymoon like everybody else."

"Why not?" She asked.

"We are a special couple God has brought together. Let's go to the Immanuel House for Blind Orphans for our honeymoon."

"The Immanuel House for Blind Orphans?" She seemed puzzled.

"That's right. That place is full of orphans and abandoned children. We've seen how they live with our own eyes. Are they not our brothers and sisters whom we must look after?" I challenged her.

"Let's do that. That will be more meaningful for us." She agreed whole heartedly.

Honeymoon at the Immanuel House Blind Orphans

After the wedding reception was over, we headed toward the Immanuel House for Blind Orphans in Suyu-Ri. Because I was able to spend the first day of my marriage with my beloved blind sisters and brothers, I believe I had the happiest and most enjoyable honeymoon possible. I got her to consent to spend our honeymoon there as a sign of her dedication to live and sacrifice her life for the good of my fellow blind brothers and sisters.

We entered the orphanage.

"Wow! It's our pastor intern with his wife!" The orphans ran out knowing I had brought my wife and started to hang on to my arms.

"How have all my cuties been?" I squealed in excitement.

We mingled with them all afternoon. Dinnertime came and we sat with the rest of the orphans to have our bowl of wheat rice with soybean soup.

The supervisor poked my side and said, "What are you doing here with your newly wed bride?"

My wife answered that one. "This must be the special menu at the Immanuel House. Now, is this Hawaiian wheat or Alaskan wheat?"

"Ah, that! That's from the Korea's No Man's Mountain." The whole room rippled with waves of laughter at the supervisor's witty remark. At that moment, a teardrop from my eyes fell into the soybean soup.

"Ah, here is a groom who thinks soybean soup is not enough for him that he has to mix it with his tears. Is this a celebration or what!?" It was then the Immanuel Choir broke into a song of celebration as they lit fire-crackers. The song was combined with the shouts of the children. It was the work of the supervisor.

Our First House: The 40,000 Won Studio

Being financially powerless, I had to walk through a field sharper thorns. We had rented a place with 40,000 as deposit. I was busy with my senior thesis at the time, so I would leave Jung-Ja at home alone for a month or more at a time as I made the final changes to my thesis in the dorm room.

My wife worked at the Immanuel House for Blind Orphans during the day, and since she was left by herself in the evenings, her parents came to stay with her. Since the fire, they were temporarily out of work. Neither of us complained. I had to spend some nights at the male professor's dorm.

After marriage, our lives became utterly disorganized. Seeing our situation, my parents-in-law blamed me from time to time. Whenever they did, all I could do was to assure them of a brighter future and encourage them to bear with us.

February of 1969, the graduation ceremony of the Presbyterian Seminary was held at Young Nak Church. Countless guests from all over the nation created a festive mood. I thanked God for the past three years for allowing me to study hard and pass all my required classes for my Masters in Divinity degree so that I may serve in the ministry for the blind.

When I was working at the Suyu-Ri Orphanage for the Blind, God opened up a new window of opportunity. A pastor came and asked me for help. The church he was pastoring was in a state of financial disorder. I accepted his offer and looked after the church with great care even in the midst of my own personal difficulties.

Around that time, my friend, Hyung-Kil Kang's mother passed away. Since he was in America studying as an international student, he was unable to return to Korea. The empty tomb was prepared on the summit of Jungneung and Miari. I rounded up all my friends and my wife, and we went to visit the mourning family. We stayed up all night praying and attended the funeral. My wife sang an eulogy and comforted the family.

To earn our living expenses, I privately tutored English and held English conversational sessions with nurses who were planning to study in America. My wife worked as a dormitory supervisor at a wig factory for several months.

I served at a non-handicapped church for a year and a half and learned through experiences some important lessons separate from the ministry. A newly planted church operating under the sole authority of the senior pastor gave me tremendous stress. Besides, there were no guarantees

The Debt of Love
I Owe to My Family

It is the dream of most women in the world to marry a man of wealth, good looks, and education. I have no idea what my wife married me for. Before I was married, I thought I would take care of my wife better than any man, and give the parental love I had never received to my children. But after marrying and having two daughters, I lacked too much to make my dream family a reality. Reality was too cold and brutal.

My wife and I experienced financial hardships after we were married. There were many times we had to satisfy our hunger with a couple of bean pastries, baked yams, or noodles from a street vendor. My wife would skip lunch but always packed my lunch. Seeing our condition, the Immanuel Orphanage supervisor gave us a bag of brown rice. We rejoiced as if we had met the Savior.

In one instance, my wife set out to be an insurance salesperson. But after a few days of not having sold a single insurance policy, she was forced to quit.

I am truly thankful that God preserved our health living in a place where fleas and bedbugs dominated, where our roof served as an ideal track for the mice to run their never ending marathons, and where the briquette gas seeped through the thin floors and walls. Why there were never any accidents when my two little children were left alone in the house all day long can only be attributed to God's protection.

During the time when our family was undergoing such hardship, I was introduced to an Englishman by Reverend Allen Clark. As I worked for the English gentleman, he planted many visions in my heart, and paid me generously.

Like God sent a crow to feed Elijah, miracles took place in my life from time to time. My wife encouraged me in hard times saying that if God was with us, we had nothing to worry about. She told me not to despair. Being only human, she too got frustrated every now and then.

My wife always said that one must be clean-cut if one wants to appeal to others. For that reason, she incessantly cleaned my ancient clothing and dressed me all nice and neat. She also read me many books that helped me greatly in my ministry. Even now, she reads me newspapers and books.

I remember some heartbreaking episodes as I reared my two daughters. In front of our house was a little store that displayed ice creams, cookies, and pastries. The kids would play near the store and when they came home, they asked, "Daddy, can you buy us some ice cream?"

"Daddy, buy us some cookies." But against their earnest solicitations, I had to deny their wishes simply because I didn't have any money to buy them such treats. Such memories have left their indelible marks of pain in the recesses of my heart. I also regretfully recall of not being able to buy them warm undergarments, coats, or fur boots during cold winters.

God brought them up so well that our oldest majored in voice and the younger in piano. They are now walking the individual paths they have chosen. My wife and daughters do not treat me as they would a blind person. They treat me as a person without a handicap. They only realize my blindness when I accidentally spill a cup of water on the floor or run into something they had placed on the table. I am so grateful that my beloved wife and daughters have treated me as they would a man without a handicap.

Doing ministry with contributions sent by churches and individual believers kept me away from spending much time with the family. Thinking that helping suffering people was the only way to pay back the generosity of my sponsors, I worked hard without looking ahead or behind. I always considered taking vacations with the family to the beaches, mountains, fields, or going to a nice restaurant and eating out with the family as something other people did. I didn't want to hide God's glory from any misunderstanding among my sponsors and coworkers about my work. However, when my daughters get married and have their own families, a great feast awaits me.

B
O
O
K

III

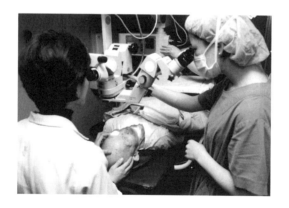

Mission Field Episodes

A Prelude of Hope to a New Ministry

I went wandering around from day to day even through the second year after the marriage. My restlessness increased even more after I failed in my attempt to study in America. My immediate concern was how to make a living to support my family. My wife worked as a director of the Immanuel Orphanage for the Blind, and I spent joyous days of teaching and meeting with students at a newly started church. The church had decided on a monthly payment of 5,000 won, but being a poor church, I was never paid. Living with my parents-in-law made the situation more difficult. Finally, my wife was offered a position as a dormitory supervisor in a public corporation in Young-Deung-Po.

In those days, I literally lived on a piece of bread and slept on a chair in one of the classrooms of the Immanuel Orphanage. I waited eagerly for Saturdays and Sundays because I forgot all my worries when I mingled with students at church. After living like that for a while, one of the teachers at the Immanuel Orphanage who knew me since I was little and had taught me Braille, perhaps thought it improper for me to sleep in the classroom in such a manner. He deadbolted the classroom, my sleeping headquarters, so I wouldn't be able to enter. I found out one hot summer night when I came back from taking care of some business. I was truly devastated.

I spent the night on a bench at the playground at the Immanuel Orphanage. Because of the national curfew, the night was completely silent; not even a mouse stirred. I sat, thought and prayed through the deep night. The sirens rang, signaling 4:00 a.m. At 4:30, the church bells rang for the early morning service. Because I had spent the night outside, I smelled of sweat and looked pitiful. Afraid someone might see me, I crouched and hid until I washed my face and went to hide behind a piano in the auditorium until I finally decided to go out.

I stole away to a bakery nearby and ordered a glass of milk and bread. As I was eating, a pastor came into the bakery with some of his church members. We exchanged greetings and chatted for a while. Then he offered me a position to teach children and youth group at his church for 6,000 won a month. My wife was earning 20,000 won a month as a dormitory supervisor at the time.

He put a condition to my coming, however. I had to move close to the church and my wife must accompany me. My wife had been away for 4 months at the time he offered me the job. I called my wife and discussed the offer with her. When I asked what she thought, she told me she would quit and come immediately. One month later, we moved close to the church.

The church ordained me as the intern pastor. I took my ordination examination while serving there. Including the early morning service and care of church members, I took on most of the administrative work at the church. As I did my very best, all children and youth as well as the young adults and the entire congregation began to favor me and follow my leadership. However, the senior pastor began to give me dirty looks indicating that he might have grown jealous of all the affection I was getting. The hymn, "There is No Rest For My Weary Soul" described my condition perfectly. Thinking this also wasn't the place for me, I resigned my internship and moved to a different church.

I was given charge of the children and youth ministry at the new church I moved to. However, the same thing happened there as well. Again, thinking this church wasn't for me, I decided to forget everything and begin a church for the blind with a friend of mine. The church we started without a single penny has now grown to 400 members. Through this experience, I was able to learn that there is hope beyond despair and a road beyond hopelessness. Although we live in a financially troubled period, water will surely spring out if we continue to dig the well of faith without despairing.

Do Not Rely on People

Everyone goes through trouble and anguish because reality doesn't always live up to your dreams. I was no exception. My grandiose dream of studying in America was shattered to pieces, and everyday life seemed vain and meaningless. Opening my eyes in the morning, I would agonize over where to go and what to do that day. With a piece of bread in my hand, there were many times I wanted to go to a quiet place where no one knew me and just cry endlessly. After filling my stomach with a bowl of brown rice without any side dishes, I would go to a canyon in Suyu-Ri and converse with the trees as I listened to the streams of water.

'When will I ever proudly step forward in this world and meet true friends? When will I ever live a life of giving and helping like others?' I pondered over a great deal of issues. While doing so, I came up with an idea. Even though I might not be able to meet with the president, I thought I could meet with the prime minister at least. I was determined to have an interview with him and explain my situation so that he would give me some money for me to start a new life. The next day, I went to the Capitol Building and begged the security guards to let me meet with the prime minister. Every time I did so, they either told me he went to the Blue House (equivalent to the White House) or that he was in a meeting. For days, I went back to the Capitol Building and insisted on meeting with the prime minister.

That drew me close to the security guards. I got to know them better as we shared ice cream and rice cookies with each other. One of the guards told me that since it's difficult to meet with the prime minister here, he advised me to go to the official residence of the prime minister in Samchun City. Taking his advice, I went to the prime minister's official residence when he would be leaving for work. But lo and behold! The security at his residence was much greater than at the capitol building.

I told them I wanted to discuss the problem of social welfare for the blind with the prime minister. They told me not to come to the official residence but to go to the Capitol Building. I told them that I had attempted to meet him there already but the guards at the Capitol Building told me to come here. Finally, when I reached the checkpoint, I explained everything. They told me the prime minister never holds interviews at the official residence, and told me to go back to the Capital Building. Innocently, I went back to the Capital Building. When I did, the guards, familiar with me by now, asked me why I had returned. I told them security was too tight at the official residence so I was unable to go in. They told me not to go there during the morning when he goes to work but in the evening when he comes back.

I had a piece of bread for lunch and circled Duksoo Place several times, waiting until the dusk. I took off toward the prime minister's official residence when the time of his return drew near. When the evening shift security guards saw a strange man, they threatened to report me to the police. Because an ill clad blind man was asking to meet with the prime minister, they treated me like some kind of a lunatic.

"I am neither a bad guy nor a lunatic. I am trying to fulfill a great dream and I'm asking to meet with the prime minister because I need his help." I clarified my motives. I didn't even have my residence card with me. The only item which proved my identity was the student ID I had kept from my seminary years. As I showed them my student ID, I told them that I would be working for the good of the nation and the society in the near future. It was only then a high official told me he had an idea.

Since the prime minister's wife stayed at the Chung-Ku residence, he told me to go see her there. He even drew me an accurate map to the place. The next morning, accompanied by one of my former students at church, we headed toward the prime minister's Chung-Ku residence. We begged the security guard to let us see the prime minister's wife. He heaped curses on us and said that he would call the police if we kept bothering him.

After visiting the Chung-Ku residence three times, I changed my mind and returned to the Capitol Building. The night before I went back to the Capitol Building, I typed up everything I wanted to say. I again went to the security office at the Capital Building the next morning. I told them who I was and asked to be admitted to the prime minister's secretary's office. One of the security guards said he was truly impressed with my effort and rang up the secretary's office for me. I entered the Capitol Building for the first time in my life and went to the secretary's office.

The ceaseless noise of the cicadas from the trees in the garden rang in my ears. I waited in front of the secretary's office for about 30 minutes. They finally told me to come in. The secretary asked me why I wanted to meet with the prime minister. I showed him the letter I had typed up all night and asked to meet with the prime minister. The secretary told me that if I left it with him, he would look it over and contact me shortly. I left the phone number of the Immanuel Orphanage and came back home. I waited and waited. There was no reply. After that, I sent out 20-30 pleading letters to the president and the prime minister, but there was still no reply. I believed everything would be fine if I could only meet with the prime minister, but that too was futile.

It was then I made a vow. Even if I had to starve many meals and only drink from mountain streams, I vowed never to depend on persons of authority. I realized that it was only when I completely depended on God through faith that my future would open up.

Today, 30 years later, it is only too ironic that I was able to carry out reforms for the nation and the society which neither the president nor the prime minister could have ever accomplished, simply because the prime minister did not meet with me at that time. If the prime minister had met with me, and given me money and granted me a job out of pity, I would

The First Step of
My Ministry for the Blind

The Birth of Korea's First United Church for the Blind

Church planting should be the priority of any mission. Likewise, the mission for the visually challenged had to start with the construction of a church devoted to them. I visited my benefactor Reverend Allen Clark.

"Reverend Clark, I need to build a church to start a mission for the blind. Can you help me?"

"There is an English missionary in Korea working with Amerasian children of mixed race. How would you like to partner up with him?"

At the time, I had an one-year-old daughter. As head of the family, I felt a heavy responsibility and burden for taking care of my family. Therefore, I was in great need of sponsors for the ministry. I went everywhere giving emphatic lectures on the importance of doing blind missions.

Once out of frustration, a few of my friends and I visited Reverend Kyung-Jik Han. We pleaded for Youngnak Church's sponsorship of our work. Reverend Han was good enough to offer up a prayer of blessing for our ministry. Strengthened by that prayer, I again ran to any place where I might receive an offering for our mission work. Finally, I was able to discuss my dreams of planting a church which would be a cornerstone to blind missions with my close friend, Reverend Suk-Kwon Park.

Frankly, since I did not attend a school for the blind like other blind people, I couldn't understand as deeply the dark reality of the visually challenged. Knowing this, Reverend Park decided that he would have personal contact with the blind, and I would be in charge of administration and publicity.

With the help of a certain blind individual, we established the United Church for the Blind. Our first worship service took place given the first week of January 1972. We were able to hold services in a Youth Group room of Chungmu Church for the next five years. However, the situation called for a change. The Chungmu Church requested us to leave. Looking for an appropriate place of worship, we found a dilapidated apartment in the area of Hwehyun. We rented it and held our service there for the next few years. Then with difficulty, we were able to obtain a single family home and soon held our services in a renovated sanctuary.

Years after that, with much persuading and contact with Youngnak Church, we built the very first church for the blind in Korea on a hill next to the entrance to the Namsan Tunnel.

As the church grew, with the cooperation of the Korea Bible Association, we were able to publish Braille Bibles. Not only did I personally distribute the braille Bibles but also did my best to provide them to every school and orphanage for the blind.

The Day of My Pastoral Ordination

While starting up the United Church for the Blind and distributing braille Bibles, I finally received my much awaited pastoral ordination in 1973. The moment the members of the ordination board laid their hands on my head to pray, I felt the strong presence of the Holy Spirit. Overcome with depth and breadth of God's love, I offered up a tearful prayer of thanksgiving. Twenty some years earlier, when I left my aunt's house, I remembered praying, "God, if you will only save me, I will become a pastor to do your work."

In answer to that prayer, God faithfully protected me as He enabled me to overcome many hardships and failures. Not only that, He also fostered leadership skills within me and gifts for ministry. After being ordained by the Board of Elders of Seoul from the General Assembly of the Presbyterian Church of Korea for the missions work to the visually challenged, the range of my ministry broadened considerably.

As soon as I received my pastoral ordination, people's perception of me changed. In 1973, the General Assembly of the Presbyterian Church of Korea established the Blind Evangelical Missions within the Evangelism Department and invited me to serve as its director. Upon my resignation as the pastor of the United Church of the Blind, my friend Reverend Park naturally took over all responsibilities, and I took my new position as the director of the Blind Evangelical Missions in the General Assembly.

How amazing all of this was. I was able to carry out the visions and programs I had prayed for during years of studying theology and ministry. The reason I had so easily accepted the offer rested on the fact that the Evangelism Department of Presbytery of the General Assembly of the Presbyterian Church of Korea set policies and carry out the missionary work for the blind. I discovered the possibility of receiving support funds from churches nationwide if a specific mission strategy could be developed.

I took charge of this important task. However, the job title 'Director of Blind Evangelical Missions' only existed in theory. In reality, it was a lonely post under the shadow of the Evangelism Department where I had to create something out of nothing. Trusting in the Bible verse, "Your beginnings will seem humble, so prosperous will your future be." (Job 8:7), I set out to find what work I had to do.

According to statistics, there are 200,000 completely blind people in Korea. Another 5,000,000 with an eyesight of 0.2 or less. I considered what we could do for them. The first thing was to send braille Bibles and hymnals to all churches, schools for the visually disabled and massage centers. The response was good. We received requests to send more and the support funds we received in return were distributed to various places.

Another project I started along with Bible distribution was providing tuition for the blind. This involved providing scholarships for those enrolled in Schools for the Visually Disabled and at the same time, placing them in appropriate educational institutions according to their gifts and talents. For those who were burning with God's calling, we sent them to seminary to receive theological training. After that, we established long-term plans for our students providing jobs for them at facilities built for the blind. Of course, if they were talented in music, we sent them to music schools and recommended that they serve in missions.

Up to 1998, for 25 years, we had provided scholarships for 900 visually challenged college students and seminarians. How can I not praise God who had used an individual like me to become like a kernel of wheat which falls to the ground to produce 30, 60, 100 times the crop?

Although I was part of the Evangelism Department of the General Assembly, that alone could not satisfy my burning passion for missions. I did not refuse any responsibility given to me but worked faithfully like a silent ox. From 1972 until the present, I have served as the social welfare organization representative director for the visually disabled. From 1972 through 1976, I was the director of the Blind Evangelical Mission. Also, from 1977 to 1978, I served as the director of the Asia Missions Conference for the Visually Disabled.

I could not limit my mission activities to Korea alone. I broadened my ministry internationally to Korean churches, mostly those in America, Japan, the Philippines and Europe. This became important because the support I was raising in Korea alone wasn't enough.

The ministry to the visually disabled that started in the doorway of room 807 of the Christian Building of the General Assembly was expanding with each passing day. I mustered courage to treat every pastor who walked through my office door with courtesy and genuine concern. With the support of the well-meaning pastors, the mood and appearance of the office started to change.

Within the General Assembly's Evangelism Department, everyone began to encourage me and offer help. I was able to hire a secretary after six months. I visited many churches with diligence, holding "Missions Night for the Visually Disabled." This helped create an association of supporters for Blind Evangelical Mission within the General Assembly's Evangelism Department. With the cooperation of the members of the presbytery, many more activities were made possible.

We once had great success throwing a nonprofit concert with the consent and participation of several church choirs. We also produced a musical that went exceedingly well. In another instance, we were allowed to have three nights of revival meetings for the visually challenged at the Young Nak Church. For the next four years, the mission activities for the blind had begun to pave the road completely. I was assured that Korean churches would actively support the Blind Evangelical Mission in the future.

From the Mission Campaign to an Eye Opening Ministry

The Feeding of the Five Thousand

The activities of the Blind Evangelical Mission mostly focused on mission conferences, bazaars, concerts, or special meetings. Such were the things that made up the missions campaign. Also, providing scholarships, fund-raising, sending out braille Bibles and hymnals to each church and giving to schools for the blind were all important ministries. However, God surprised me greatly by opening wide the window to direct involvement with the medical mission of restoring sight to the blind.

In 1977, a very important guest visited the Evangelism Department. Professor Jung-Soon Lee, who was the professor of home economics in Chungbuk College, came along with my friend, Ki-Chul Park. She took out an envelope from her bag, and without hesitation, handed it to me.

She said, "Pastor, I want to give sight to the visually disabled. I was saving this money for my son's wedding, but I hope you can use it for operations." At that moment, a volcanic eruption of heartfelt emotion gave me a sudden chill. I firmly grabbed Professor Lee's hand as tears of overwhelming emotion streamed down my cheeks. Professor Lee was left alone with her son when her husband was kidnapped to the North. She had brought a sum equaling $8,000 she had been saving for her son's wedding.

The story behind the medical offering went like this: One day, Professor Lee was visiting a School for the Blind in Chungju. As she was having a good time with the blind students, she happened to notice a white covering over the pupil of one of the student's eyes. After careful observation, she came to the conclusion that if only someone would remove that veil for her, she would be able to see clearly. A conviction surged up within her troubled heart like a burning flame.

Even up to that point, no specific plans had been made to offer surgical eye operations to the blind. But Professor Lee's request became the starting point of medical mission for the visually disabled. The medical mission for the 200,000 blind and 5 million partially blind was started with this woman's special offering.

Immediately upon receipt of her precious offering, I met with several opthomologists. I asked if it was possible for a blind person to regain sight through an eye operation. They all responded that it was —the only problem would be the cost. Through such means, the very first sight restoration operation took place with Professor Lee's offering. We laid a brother on the operating table and prayed over him.

"God who restores sight to the blind, and enables one to see the world again, we are about to begin our first eye operation having been led by Your call. Please have mercy on us and grant us the light of Your healing. Please steady the hands of those who will be performing the operation and let their work truly be a holy ministry which glorifies You."

The Success of the First Eye Operation

The result of the first operation was more than satisfactory. The brother who received the operation had his sight restored in a few days. Greatly impressed with the success, the Mission Association for the Blind started planning various strategies from every possible angle to publicize the eye operation on a grander scale. Since the operation was little known to the people at the time, I brought more publicity to it by traveling from one church to another.

After the initial success, these operations slowly continued with the help of a few optometrists, hospitals and well-meaning supporters. Such amazing news traveled nationwide through newspaper stories. The success of these stories became known as the 'Miracle of Siloam" as it gathered interest from many churches. After that, a full-scale, nation-wide campaign for eye operations was launched.

The Kitok Kongbo, newspaper of the Presbyterian Church published by the Korean Presbytery reported extensively, publicizing the 'Eye Operation of Love Campaign' in every issue. They published all the local news and responses they had received concerning the campaign as well as precise and detailed news from mission organizations located in America, Canada, Japan, Germany, and the Middle East. The response began to increase. Finally, the newspaper gave its full support to the eye operation movement for its 50th Anniversary Mission Campaign.

It would be impossible to relate the entire campaign. The offerings from churches totaled up to 300 thousand *won*(approximately US $600). Once such an offering was sent in, other offerings from all levels of society and other organizations started to flow in. Not only did they give offerings for the operations, they sent in hundreds of thousands of won to purchase necessary equipment and build facilities for the operation.

From then until now, there have been an numerous people who were able to regain sight due to successful operations. I cannot even begin to express my overwhelming gratitude to God. I would like to share the joy and success of these medical missions with many believers, and churches as well as others who have gladly and faithfully contributed to restoring sight to their beloved brothers and sisters to this day.

There still remain thousands of countless people waiting to have their sight restored. We continue to hold a worldwide eyesight recovery operation campaign so that one by one, they may open their eyes. For this purpose I race to any place that calls me at any time. Whenever an operation is a success, the entire staff of the Siloam Eye Hospital offers up thanksgiving and praise of joy. The 2000-year-old story of the man who was sent to the Spring of Siloam and regained his sight continues to this day at the Siloam Eye Hospital.

"While I am in the world, I am the light of the world." Having said this, he spit on the ground, made some mud with the saliva, and put it on the man's eyes. "Go," he told him, "wash in the Pool of Siloam" (this word means 'Sent'). So the man went and washed, and came home seeing."

(John 9:5-7)

The Lesson I Learned from the Rehabilitation Training Center

Enrollment in the Chicago Rehabilitation Center
for the Visually Handicapped

Although there are a great many episodes, I will never forget in my life, the most memorable is this one.

From 1976, as I toured internationally for the ministry and social welfare, I was able to learn and experience firsthand certain things regarding the rehabilitation of the visually handicapped in different cultures. In 1980, with the recommendation of my friend, Reverend Hyung-Kil Kang who was pastoring a church in Chicago, I had the opportunity to receive training from the Illinois state-operated Rehabilitation Center for the Visually Handicapped located in the city of Chicago.

I was very curious about condition of the blind in America: how they lived, how American society taught independence to the blind, and how they handled the information regarding the entire rehabilitation training program.

I enrolled in the Rehabilitation Center for the Visually Handicapped. The center enrolled only a few severely blind people from all over the states. It was a gathering of various people, from managers of well known corporation to an ex-governor, even a pilot; but I was the first Asian to enroll in the history of their program.

Just as I had heard, all the facilities were simply perfect. It was heaven on earth. Because the content and structure of their program was based on a perfectly crafted system of education, people were able to receive appropriate counsel according to one's level. A group of five people were assigned to each instructor. From cooking to finding the right path, the content of the lessons varied. It took about two years to learn everything needed to lead an independent life.

My instructor was a single lady who received her masters from Michigan University and was a deacon at the First Presbyterian Church. During the week-long orientation, the instructor called me to her office. She told me that the school required students to take a test to continue their studies after the one week of free lodging and meals. However, being the first Asian to enroll in the program, she was concerned about what questions she should put on the test.

Philippians 4:13 came to my mind: "I can do everything through Him who gives me strength.". Thinking about that verse, I told her that whatever questions I received, I can do it. She stared at me for a long time. She kept repeating, "Are you sure?" I answered affirmatively. We agreed to meet at a designated place after lunch. She told me to wear a warm coat and gloves.

The Strange Entrance Exam

I promptly went to the appointed spot. The instructor said, "You are a clergyman as well as a Christian. You must take full responsibility for your words. Therefore, you may remain in this school and continue with your education if you pass today's test. However, if you fail, you must return to Korea. What's your answer?"

I told her I would take the test as promised. Then the instructor gave me a thick cane and told me to lead the way. I did as she said. She followed behind me as she put me through the test. I don't like canes very much. Because I did not carry a cane with me regularly, I felt embarrassed the moment I held the cane in my hand. But how could I refuse when I had come to learn?

The instructor told me to go right, left, and forward as we walked for fifteen minutes. We came to a bus station. We waited for a while and the bus finally arrived. We rode on that bus for about 40 minutes while the instructor explained many things to me.

We finally got off at a bus stop. She stood me on the sidewalk and coldly repeated that I must keep my word since I am a minister. She said, "I am going to leave you here. If you find your way back to the school any way you can, I will pass you and let you study for another year or two. If you cannot find your way back, you have no choice but to return to your own country." With that, she was gone.

Everything happened so suddenly; I felt a kind of despair. I stood there, dismally. I didn't know the area or how to get on a bus. No matter how much I thought about it, I couldn't think of any good ideas.

At that moment, the Holy Spirit gave me wisdom. I prayed, "Lord, please give me wisdom since I am faced with yet another test in my life." Then the answer came, "Take the staff in your hand and wave it in the road."

Immediately, I entered the traffic and started to wave my cane. Although I knew that there were many passing cars right in front of my eyes and that this was a very dangerous venture, I could only wait since all I did was obey the guidance of the Holy Spirit. I was convinced that somebody was going to help me.

The drivers in the passing cars screamed, "Are you crazy?!" Many cars passed me by. Out of those cars, one car finally stopped and the drivers kindly asked, "How can I help you?" He waited patiently for my answer. I was delighted. I gave him the address of the rehabilitation center. "I would be ever so grateful if you could take me there." I told him. He gladly consented to my request and ushered me into his car. We talked about this and that while he drove. The kind warm gentleman was a Catholic Priest. He led me all the way to the Rehabilitation Center and left me with words of encouragement.

Having arrived at the school, I waited for my instructor at the entrance. She showed up one hour after my return. The reason being I came by car and she returned by bus.

As soon as she saw me, she jumped up and down. She couldn't stop repeating the word, "Wonderful! Wonderful!" She asked me, "How did you get here so fast?" I told her I got back safely because the Holy Spirit had sent someone to me. Without a doubt, I passed the test. The next morning, during the first lecture, she introduced me to the students.

"Reverend Sun-Tae Kim is a pastor from Korea who has wonderfully passed his exam. He is truly a genius among us students. Therefore, I instruct you to learn everything you need to learn about independent living from him."

I didn't know how to react to the thunderous applause. From that day forth, I received all the love and popularity from every teacher and student. I became the center of interest and attention. Since my instructor said I was a genius, one of the students touched my head and ears. There was even a lady who joked she would marry me if I was single.

From Monday to Friday, I received regular lessons, and from Friday afternoon until Sunday, I did ministry tasks with my friend, Reverend Hyung-Kil Kang. Since I had received such a great welcome from the Korean-American churches as well as a large honorarium, I invited all the teachers and students to a Korean restaurant and threw a huge party for them. I explained and introduced them to Korean food as well as its culture and music.

The regular course took about 1-2 years to complete. However, I finished in five months with A's. Having been impressed with the rehabilitation program in Chicago, I made a vow to establish such a center for the visually handicapped once I got back to Korea. The vow was fulfilled in 1997 when the four-story "House of Light" was built across from the Siloam Eye Hospital.

My Interest in the Psychology of the Visually Disabled

Although I had learned a lot from the classes I took at the Chicago Rehabilitation Center, I realized the importance of mental attitude and social interests. The area which held my interest the most was the psychology of visually handicapped people. For the visually handicapped, psychological insecurities can often produce mental disorders or feeling of complete helplessness where the personality is destroyed; resulting in severe dementia. Alternately, the blind can experience an unbearable weight of guilt which leads to self-abuse and destruction. They might try to sever all ties and contact from people in an attempt to escape from society. Such situations pose a serious problem.

Therefore, well-prepared centers to educate the visually handicapped for a healthier and better functioning life are needed. I believe a social welfare system or training centers where the blind will not fall into depression but where they can find their own life-style are truly invaluable. In order to complement the weaknesses of the visually handicapped, rehabilitation centers need to offer career training. Not only does the career training have to be versatile, but it must be given by qualified professors who will lead them into the right career as well as give them a wide range of job opportunities.

As I observed the cheerful attitudes of the students who received training with me at the Chicago Rehabilitation Center, I desperately wished that visually handicapped people in Korea would soon receive fair education opportunities from the government—especially the chance to receive rehabilitation training. In order for Korea to become a country where every citizen is guaranteed his or her rights, it must first recognize its need to transform society's attitudes toward the handicapped. Such convictions reverberate through my bones.

The Day of International Humiliation

Receiving an Invitation from the United Church of Christ in Japan

If I were to list all the names of churches and social services I have visited in doing missionary work for the visually handicapped, we would run out of pages. And if I were to list every individual I have met in relation to my ministry, the list would go on infinitely. The types of meetings were unique as well.

However, all my efforts in attending those conferences and meeting those people were focused on one thing only; to raise funds for blind missions. Since 1973, holding the office of director at the Blind Evangelical Mission of the General Assembly, the range of my activities were incredibly wide and even risky for the last twenty-five years. There were a countless number of conferences where I gave my testimony—conferences geared toward all churches nationwide. I am thankful to God for the guidance of the Holy Spirit and the support of believers who came together to help our mission in every one of those meetings.

I visited the Korean-Japanese Church in Japan to raise funds needed for our evangelism ministry and to buy equipment for our Siloam Eye Hospital. But my first visit to Japan was to collect data regarding rehabilitation programs, social services, and other benefits they offered to the visually handicapped in Japan.

I was invited by the United Church of Christ in Japan. However, it was very difficult to receive a visa to enter Japan at that time. I had to first receive an official invitation before applying for a passport. It was a difficult and painstaking process after which one had to go through an exhaustive background check. Such process took the entire day. Just that period lasted a good three months. After receiving a passport, in order to get a visa, one was required to undergo inspection by the Ministry of Justice in Japan. Therefore, the entire process took about half a year.

The Incident at Kimpo International Airport

March 19, 1976. After passing a long screening process, and after receiving my passport and visa, I was finally on my way to Japan. The representatives from the United Church of Christ who had invited me, along with members of the Japan Blind Mission Association were supposed to meet me at Haneda Airport in Japan. Overcome with the emotion of my first international trip and the prospect of getting on a plane, I was overly excited.

After going through all the necessary procedures, I was about to pass through the final departure gate. I handed my passport to the inspector. He looked at my passport and said he couldn't permit my departure because I had not fulfilled my military duty. He refused to let me through even though the passport clearly stated that I was blind and my registration card had 'handicapped' written on it making it obvious that I couldn't serve in the military.

While I argued with the inspector, the long line of passengers screamed and shouted at me to hurry up. The inspector even threatened to sue me to securities for interfering with his duties. Without a choice, I went to the manager in charge of all arrivals and departures at the Ministry of Justice. I pleaded with him to let me on the plane because if I missed the flight today, I would be internationally humiliated. After looking over my travel documents, he told me there was absolutely no problem with my departure. He sent me back to the inspector.

I went back to that young inspector, but he rejected me nevertheless. While all that was going on, the flight took off. The situation was so ridiculous. For the first time, I was about to become an international figure, but I first had to endure international humiliation. Such ignorant people like these probably still exist today. People like that bring shame to civilized societies.

I later heard that the members of the Blind Mission Association waited for me late into the night. Although the plane had already taken off, I still needed to get a certificate of exemption from military duties. I had no idea how one would get such a thing. My wife and I returned home feeling empty. I researched this matter, and everyone told me that the action of the inspector was completely unacceptable.

Early the next morning, I went to an Ophthalmologist and received a diagnosis. I immediately applied for the certificate of exemption from military duty at the military office. Even there, they couldn't figure out why the inspector did not allow my departure and handed me the certificate. I finally received permission to depart and got on a plane for the first time in my life on March 20, 1976.

When I met with the members of the Blind Missions Association in Japan, I asked for forgiveness more than a hundred times. I didn't know what to do out of embarrassment and guilt. It was a relief that they viewed the incident as a spiritual obstacle to mission work for the blind.

I received a warm welcome from the members of the association at Haneda Airport and, with their mediation, I visited some of the facilities for the visually handicapped. From the airport to the city, the streets were covered with guiding braille letters. The signs were also written in braille letters. Whether buying a train ticket or going to the bathroom, I was surprised at the clear directions and signs placed so the blind could easily get around. Many visually challenged people were freely roaming the streets. Also, they could easily purchase train or bus tickets and safely reach their destination. When I compared that to the condition of Korea's care for the blind, the differences were immense. I imagined how much work needed to be done in our country.

There was another surprising facility. When I came to the crosswalk, I heard a beautiful song. I asked my guide about it, and he told me that the song was a signal to cross the road. I imagined how wonderful it was to have the non-handicapped crossing the road to the sound of the music along with the visually handicapped. It was a beautiful picture indeed. Fortunately, our country has also installed such systems at the crosswalks since 1981. Perhaps it was due to the influence of its neighboring country.

I visited Shinjuku near Tokyo. There I visited the city-operated library for the blind and Career Rehabilitation Center for the Blind, as well as various acupuncture businesses run by the visually handicapped. The streets there were also covered with the braille letters, and on every corner, bells were installed so that their ringing would prevent the blind from losing their direction. Such amenities existed throughout the country. They were obviously adopted from America. The thought that if I worked with every fiber of my being, I might cause Korea to adopt such amenities for the blind made my blood boil with excitement and great expectation.

As I visited the library and the rehabilitation centers, I spent many hours listening to reports and discussing with the head of those facilities. Through my interactions, I received many new ideas and collected necessary information for my ministry. The most important thing I learned was the faithful attitude of each volunteer worker serving the blind; they were like a family.

Although they weren't Christians, it was truly amazing how they showed love to the blind through built-in kindness and service. I thought that the blind born in Japan must be very happy.

The Reason Why Our Country is Behind in Its Accommodations for the Visually Disabled

But why is it that the living conditions and treatment of the blind in Korea lag so far behind Japan? First, we must re-evaluate the prejudice our society has against the visually handicapped. There have been many parents who, upon the birth of a blind child, thought that the family had been cursed as punishment for their sins from the past life, and abandon the baby in front of a school for the blind. The thought of having received punishment for the sins of a previous life has been passed down like a custom.

Quite a few merchants label the blind unlucky and spit on them if they see them early in the morning. However, every citizen has the right to recognize the basic rights of the others; and therefore, wrong customs and superstitions must be rectified.

There is another important reason why society's attitudes about the visually handicapped cannot be reformed or developed so easily. That is because there exists those vile individuals, who like deeply-rooted poison mushrooms, take advantage of and manipulate the physical and economic weakness of the blind.

They view the visually handicapped as means to their own success and profit. With such thoughts, they even trample on the basic rights of such handicapped people. Although I have heard of stories of people who have earned great sums of money through instrumentalizing the blind, I have never heard of an instance where they used that money to build libraries, rehabilitation centers or social facilities for the blind. The very reason why our society is so backwards lies in here.

Take America for example. About 500 visually challenged people have professional careers in the field of law. More than 1000 are college professors.

A House Representative in Germany has a handicapped member. We sometimes see him on TV as he approaches the National Assembly Building in his wheelchair.

Even in our neighboring country, Japan, there are people with handicaps who are in the politics, but I have yet to hear of a person with a handicap in our country's political scene.

Within Korean churches, they collect offerings for the handicapped. However, if they neglect using the offering for the good of the handicapped, this too must be changed. Unfortunately, we cannot deny that such things are happening in our churches—it really breaks my heart. In the name of helping the visually handicapped, churches establish anonymous organizations. However, when they actually raise a considerable amount of money, they do not offer any help to the blind. Such unethical actions deceive one's faith and conscience and therefore, must be criticized harshly by society.

Especially if a leader of a church has been involved in such evil as this, he should not be able to avoid sharp and dishonorable criticism from the public unless he completely turns away from his actions and repents of it wholeheartedly.

Japan's Bullet Train

The Voluntary Vacation of Hardship

After the initial difficult trip to Japan, more and more opportunities arose to visit the churches under the United Church of Christ of Japan. With my handicap, traveling without a cane often gets me into unimaginably difficult situations. This too, I consider as an experience I must go through not for myself but for my mission.

In 1993, I had a chance to visit Japan again. After a speaking engagement at the Tokyo Korean Church, I was scheduled to lead the gathering at the Nagoya Church. Luckily, the church's senior pastor, Reverend Yi-Sang Hwang was in Tokyo for a conference. It was decided that we would travel together to his church from Tokyo by the *shinkansen*, Japan's bullet train.

I met him at the YMCA. After a cup of tea, he escorted me all the way to the Tokyo Train Station. There, we bought our tickets. At the time, I was carrying two very heavy suitcases. When we arrived at the station, he politely offered to carry one of my bags. I refused profusely thinking it would be too much of a burden on him. Not only was he escorting me, he invited me to speak at his church and even agreed to give an offering for the Siloam Eye Hospital. Those favors were more than enough. Because I was so thankful for everything already, I thought the least I could do was carry my own bags.

I slung one bag over on my shoulder and held the other in the hand of the same arm. With my free hand, I held onto Reverend Hwang's arm. It was only after we had arrived at the platform of the *shinkansen* I was able to set the bags down and rest. Because it was well past dinnertime, we tried to get on a train that had a dining cart. But while waiting for it, we ended up missing three other trains. We decided just to board one without the luxury of dining.

But there was a problem. Since our assigned seats were way in the back, we had to walk through several compartments. Sweat started to drip from my entire body and I was getting a fever. Since I was carrying the bags, I would trip over some seats and just had the hardest time following Reverend Hwang. I heard such words as "poor guy" or "pitiful" in Japanese as I walked through the compartments.

Although it was hard, I was happy as I entertained the thought that I could deliver the message of the gospel to God's beloved people. That was a comforting thought. Also, when I thought about being able to provide eyesight recovery operations from the special offering because of sharing the gospel, my present troubles didn't seem to matter.

"Reverend Hwang, how much longer do we have to go?" Whenever I asked him this, he responded, "Just a little more, just a little more." But he kept on walking with my right hand in his. For a moment, it seemed as though the excruciating pain would continue forever. When we finally sat down in our seats, I felt I had found an oasis in the desert. I slowly massaged my arm and my fingers that were carrying the bags.

I couldn't let him know I was hurting. I had a difficult time trying to cover up my pain with cheerful remarks. Shortly after sharing a simple dinner-box, we arrived at the Nagoya Church.

The Cordial Welcome I Received at the Nagoya Church

There were two rooms on the fourth floor of the Nagoya Church. I unpacked my bags in one of the rooms. That room was used weekly by the Woman's Group for meetings and just for relaxing. Early in the morning, after an hour of prayer, I turned on the faucet to wash my face. It produced no hot water; the water heater was probably out of order. Februaries in Japan are quite cold, so I didn't want to wash with cold water. I wet the towel and placed it on the heater but it was futile. Having no other choice, I washed my face with cold water and wiped my face with a towel. My face started to pulsate with heat. The thought of returning home dominated me, but I reminded myself I had to stay here for a couple more days.

An elderess arrived at the church and inquired after my well being. Delighted to see her, I blurted out, "Please turn on the hot water." Surprised, she immediately called the janitor and I had hot water within ten minutes. After that, I stayed in the room very comfortably for the next few days. However, the pain in my left shoulder and arm worsened. Whenever the pain returned, I held my arm and prayed. I still feel the pain sometimes even now.

On Sunday, I preached for the first, second and evening services and, whenever I had the chance, I spent time in fellowship with members of the church. Through informal conversations, I shared stories about the Siloam Eye Hospital. An elder who had donated equipment to the hospital was present. I thanked him for donating such wonderful equipment to our hospital. "As a result, many people were able to receive eyesight recovery operations and even rehabilitation training," I told him. I then turned my attention to another elder and challenged, "Elder Lee, why don't you do something nice for the hospital as well?" He responded, "Sure, why not?" and said he would donate surgery equipment. Tears of gratitude filled my eyes. The embarrassment and hardship I experienced on the train and the pain in my shoulder and arm meant nothing to me. I received the offering on Sunday and left the next day. My heart burned with the desire to deliver the donation to the Siloam family.

Sympathetic Love

The Definition

It took a great deal of time for me to understand the "sympathetic Christ"—the term the author of Hebrews used to depict Jesus. 'Sym' is a prefix that means 'same', and 'pathy' means 'feeling.' Together, they mean 'to feel with' something or someone.

In Chinese characters, the word offers an excellent translation. Literally, it would be translated 'compassion for the body', which does not convey the meaning well. A deeper meaning would suggest the bodily sharing of pain and suffering. It would mean 'distribution of pain.' Therefore, every missionary and minister should be an imitator of Christ and must embody the love of Christ by sharing in His suffering. I confess that the path of ministry I have walked has been so rough and brutal that I would have never passed through without the sympathizing love of Christ.

Leave With a Determination to be Martyred

In January of 1987 during the Lunar New Year's, a Korean national holiday, all the businesses were closed and travelers crowded the streets. Mid-afternoon, I was headed to the Airport to board a plane for Japan. Having over exerted myself during the holidays, I had the flu and was exhausted. Although I rarely get sick when I do, I suffer three times more than normal people do.

I thought I might miss my scheduled churches in Japan because of my illness. I had received a flu shot several days before and started to take cold medication, but to no avail. My cold did not subside that easily.

At dawn, my alarm clock went off and driven by an obsession to do what I promised, I tried to get up. My head rattled, my legs trembled and screams resounded in my ears. It was so agonizing and painful. Trying to stand up, leaning against the wall, all strength was drained from my body. It felt like I was falling down a very steep cliff. I wanted to give up. I lay down and closed my eyes. Opening them again, it was two hours later. My body was weak. I wanted to call the church in Tokyo, but I heard a soft whisper from the depths of my heart, "Are you really an evangelist? If you are, you would do your very best even to martyrdom." I froze as my finger was about to dial the number. "Lord, you are right. Your words are correct. Even though I received the call to spread your word, I dreamt of going to Tarsus like Jonah. Lord, I will go though I perish."

In the midst of dialing, I burst into tears. I had been close to denying

God's sympathetic love. I calmed my nerves and with a great determination, headed to the airport. Two elders were waiting to escort me to the airport. As I got in the car, I remarked, "Today is New Year's and here you are spending it at the airport."

"Then what about you? Are you getting on a plane on New Year's Day?" The three of us laughed. The cold wind cut through my body like a knife. Every joint in my body ached and my legs were shaking. I wanted to collapse to the floor. No matter how much I tried to keep a clear head, my whole body was on fire with a fever and I broke out in a cold sweat.

The two elders led me to the airport restaurant and I drank some juice hoping to feel better but nothing helped. Boarding time came and I went through security and dumped myself on the plane. Even in the airplane, I did not recover full consciousness. As the plane rose, a painful, desperate moaning slipped from my lips, "God, please help me."

I felt my neighboring passenger's stare at me, but I did not care. I dozed off in pain. When I opened my eyes, we were landing in Tokyo. The pastors were waiting to greet me. I explained my situation to them and they said, "You should have called if you were so sick."

"I tried to but the Holy Spirit stopped me," I responded honestly.

"There must be some amazing blessing waiting for us at this conference." Reverend Kim grabbed my hand firmly. The warmth of his hands was comforting. He led me to my lodgings, a traditional Japanese *tatami* room. I longed for Korea's warmly heated floors, but I wasn't in Korea anymore. Although geographically close, Japan was culturally very different.

I spent the first night wallowing in pain and involuntary moaning. As the cold wind seeped through the window, I felt as if the shadow of death was upon me. I thought, at what seemed like the last moment of my life, of dried radish leaf soup. Perhaps the signs of a faint appetite indicated the road to recovery.

Please Be a Good Neighbor

I persevered through the shaking and suppressed my coughs to preach twice in the morning. The message was, "Who is the true neighbor of the man who met the robbers?" I delivered the message under the strong conviction of the Holy Spirit.

"There are many brothers and sisters today groaning for this reason or that as if they have met a robber. People face to face with a robber cannot escape from the deadly situation by themselves. They need the help of a good neighbor. I believe visually challenged people are part of this group which has encountered robbers. Let us listen to the voice of our Lord today. For us to live the life of true Christianity, we must not ignore our close neighbors, but care for them with love."

With scattered coughs, quietly sharing the message, I started to hear an "amen" from here and there. I don't know how I finished the morning message. After the service, I raced to another church. As the service ended around four, I felt my body being sucked into a fiery abyss.

The church members told me they were deeply moved and wanted to question me about the Siloam Eye Hospital. Because I had come with the determination to be martyred for Christ, I ignored my pain and explained the history of our hospital and its mission statement. The question and answer session went on for more than an hour and showed no sign of closure. The head pastor finally spoke on my behalf. "It's too much for Reverend Kim to continue this meeting since he is suffering greatly from a fever. It is best to end now."

That night, I didn't get a wink of sleep. I winced in pain throughout the night. I desperately waited for arrival of the morning. To my sick body, the night in Tokyo felt long and cold. I praised and prayed through the Psalm I had memorized. "Oh Lord, You have searched me and you know me. You know when I sit and when I rise; You perceive my thoughts from afar. You discern my going out and my lying down; you are familiar with all my ways..." (Psalm 139:1-3). After I memorized the first fourteen verses, I closed my eyes. In the morning, I was able to have breakfast with the senior pastor.

The Fruit, Which Blossomed Amidst the Pain

While resting in the church office after having breakfast with the senior pastor, a woman came in to see me.

"My dear sister, what prompts you to visit me so early in the morning?" I asked.

"I came because I wanted to give something to the Siloam Hospital," she said. She gave an envelope to the senior pastor. "Although it's only a small amount, please use it for those who have encountered robbers. I would like to help as much as possible." It was an overwhelming amount. I could not hold back the tears.

I held her hands and prayed, "Lord, through the care of good neighbors who love you, it is possible to create a kingdom where people who have met robbers can be healed. Please refine this sister's precious faith as you would a heavenly jewel so that her life may be blessed."

We were able to install much needed equipment for surgery with her precious offering. The doctors had been requesting equipment for a long time, but we had to hold off due to financial reasons. Now, it was taken care of with her offering. It is written that there is no forgiveness without bloodshed. Sharing in the sympathetic love of our God produced a beautiful result.

The Story Behind the Establishment of the Siloam Eye Hospital

The Testimony of a Little Girl

In December 1981, the Siloam Mother's Association decided to hold a charity concert at what was known as the 'celebrity church'. The ministry started through this concert proved to be a stepping-stone in the establishment of a non-profit eye hospital in our country. That Hospital, of course, was Siloam. The audience that filled the church was moved to flood the place with tears as they listened to various music programs and testimonies. I prayed wholeheartedly, "With the encouragement of your love, Lord, please bless this time so that a miracle of love may happen for the ministry of the visually handicapped." Fervently praying, I was tormented by the pain which pressed my heart.

One sister began her testimony. She had gained sight after four long procedures. "My beloved Brothers and Sisters! I had suffered from natural cataracts from birth and lived a life of blindness all my life. I lived from day to day with the love and assistance of my parents, but I always wondered in my heart, 'When will I ever see this world?'

"Then one day, I heard delightful news. I could regain my sight with an operation. I received the operation sponsored by the Blind Evangelical Mission. I was afraid at first. I was doubtful if the doctors could really make me see, but like I have always done, I trusted in the Lord and received the surgery.

"After several operations, I was able to see the world little by little. My heart beat with excitement. All the accumulated sorrow burst forth. Tears of joy streamed down my face. 'Oh, thank you God! I love you Lord who has opened my eyes!'"

The sister shared her joy in receiving sight. Although I couldn't see her brightly shining eyes, I could feel them by the hot tears that poured down along with the wild applause of the crowd. One girl's testimony had brought about a miracle of love.

The CEO of a company was present that night along with his wife. They were touched by the girl's testimony. After several meetings discussing the condition of the visually handicapped with me, he and I were of one mind to establish a hospital for the blind. The CEO appealed to his employees to cooperate in the undertaking.

Here is the Miracle of Feeding of the Five Thousand

In April 1982, the miracle of erecting a specialized hospital of optometry took place. It took the work of several men to establish the hospital. They personally carried out fund raising for the project and poured all of their strength in finding the right place for the hospital. We purchased a piece of land owned by one of the founding members, but many difficulties had to be overcome in the process.

Contrary to the chairman of the board's wish, the hospital turned into a heart-disease foundation. I suffered much heartache because of this issue. However, I was ready to overcome any obstacle because I was determined to pour my heart into the realization of this miracle. After four long years, the Siloam Eye Hospital was opened as a three-story building with all the basic facilities necessary for eye operations.

Lord, I believe in the miracle of love.
The miracle of love that fed five thousand people
With five loaves of bread and two fish
Had taken place inside the Siloam Hospital.
We have been humbled by the amazing deed
you have accomplished
With the gathering of poor hearts who love You.
Another miracle you will accomplish for us awaits us.
It is the miracle of tasting the heavenly joys
As a multitude of people rush in to have their physical eyes opened.
Lord, may You be glorified.

-A prayer entry from 'Miracle of Love'

Miracle Gives Birth to Miracle

The miracles kept happening through the establishment of the Siloam Eye Hospital. We were able to open 30 patient rooms and expand the building to four stories. Initially, because we didn't have an elevator, many blind students fell down the stairs, and senior citizens had to rest several times before reaching the third floor. Now, with the addition of the Siloam House of Light, we installed an elevator between the two buildings and solved the problem. Such construction was made possible through God's miracles. Although there were difficulties in the beginning, many visually handicapped people were able to receive excellent treatment here. I believe the miracle of Siloam Jesus performed has been passed on to today. Various miracles continue to take place.

A patient with amputated legs due to bone marrow cancer who lost sight due to cataracts regained sight; eleven sisters and brothers from one family all found light from the darkness; a deaf, mute and blind boy who suffered from diabetes from birth regained sight through our hospital, enabling him to travel to places on his own. Such memorable and joyful events took place at Siloam.

The Siloam medical team, imitating the love of Christ who came to us in flesh to declare His salvation, also visited Schools for the Blind to diagnose those who were suffering from blindness. Out of those diagnosed, we would choose patients who had a chance of seeing through surgery. For those students, we provided round trip expenses to come to the Siloam

Eye Hospital and receive a free operation. Over the last thirteen years, 10,000 people have had their sight restored and heard the gospel. Such results must definitely be considered truly precious in the history of Korean mission work.

During a person's lifetime, we experience not only good and worthwhile times, but also times of misery, agony, distress and sorrow. There was a time I experienced such heartache as I worked at Siloam Hospital.

Two years had passed since the establishment of the hospital. One day, a member of the Kernel of Wheat Organization that supported our ministry, brought a very small, emaciated blind girl to us. The girl had been born blind and her family hid her in the back room, preventing her from having any ties with the outside world. They gave her one meal a day, just enough food to maintain her life. She was malnourished to the point of becoming deaf and mute with serious developmental problems. If they had paid attention to her and had she received eye treatment, there was a possibility her sight could have been restored. If something was put into her hand, she didn't know what it was; unless bread was put into her mouth, she didn't know it was edible.

Although she looked about eight, we were told she was eighteen. How much they must have abused and starved her because she was blind. If I had the money, I would have taken her into my custody and educated her, and given her ample food so that she would have regained her health. In my heart, I still regret not having known her earlier. I don't know whether she is alive or dead today, but when I think of her, my heart is pained and tears come to my eyes. Living at my aunt's house, I remember hiding in the backyard as they abused and tormented me. Such memories added to the sorrow I felt for her.

I will never forget another episode. It was January of 1994. After the morning devotions, I came up from the chapel. In the entrance stood an elderly lady and a young woman holding a baby. It looked like they were waiting for somebody. The weather being so cold, I invited them into my office and started a conversation.

The woman was the daughter-in-law of the elderly woman. They had traveled for more than three days to come here. The baby was born a year a half before. After seven or eight months, the baby had much discharge from her eyes and her pupils turned red. Living in a town without an eye doctor, they visited an old man who practiced acupuncture. The old man, who practiced without a license, prescribed collecting urine and putting it in the baby's eyes twice a day. They did as they were told, but instead of getting better, the eyes got bloodshot and the condition worsened.

As they spent anxiety filled days, they heard about the Siloam Eye Hospital on the radio. After thinking about it for a few days, they decided to visit. Immediately following the meeting, we did an extensive test on the baby's eyes. They were in the beginning stages of conjunctivitis. Had they not inserted urine into her eyes but instead given the right medication, her eyes would have healed completely. However, due to the urine, the eye structure had already melted away and even her eardrums were im-

174

paired. She also suffered from infantile cerebral paralysis. She ended up with three different handicaps.

Having found out the test results, the mother and the grandmother cried uncontrollably and endlessly. Such a scene was unbearable to watch. I managed to calm them down and prayed with them. I gave them a small gift with an adequate amount for travel expenses. As I sent them away, I told them to come back when the child grew up.

I can still hear the mother's frantic sobs. For a while that incident did not leave my mind whether I was sleeping or praying. I had a hard time concentrating on my work as a result of that event.

Starting Free Diagnosis in the Remote Islands and Rural Farming Areas

A little after that episode, we received a calling from God during prayer to go to remote islands and rural farming areas to give free diagnosis and treatment. God gave us such a calling through that little baby. We continued to pray about our concerns. We held a prayer meeting with those believers and pastors who were interested in a ministry for remote islands and rural farming areas.

The future looked gloomy for such a project. We needed manpower and medical tools; we needed medicine; we needed transportation. We had none of them. Relying on "I can do all things through Him who gives me strength," I initiated the movement with full force. Maybe because it was something that was so desperately needed and something we had to do, God helped us.

Although we asked all church denominations for help, there wasn't much response. We didn't despair and continued to pray. God finally granted us a nine-passenger van through the SBS Seoul Broadcasting Station, The Cultural Foundation, and collaboration of some churches.

This marked the beginning of our ministry to provide free eye diagnosis, eye operations, and blindness prevention to the remote islands and rural farming areas. 1995 marked the first year of this ministry, which is still currently active in doctorless villages.

B
O
O
K

IV

Unforgettable Stories and
Other Thoughts

My Partners in the
Ministry for the Blind

Friends Who gave me Hope and Courage

I started my ministry for the blind with some close friends while I was serving at Chungmu Church while Reverend Tae Jun Hwang was the associate pastor. After that, Reverend Hwang flew away to America. Once when I visited him at Jacksonville Florida. I remember it being the beginning of July 1984, when he took me to the famous Swany River.

Before I visited the river, I imagined a beautiful place. However, when I got there, my image was shattered to a million pieces in a matter of seconds. It was because the Swany Beach was crowded with mosquitoes and bugs, and the edges of the water shone with incredibly dull colors. I suppose it must have been very clean about a hundred years ago. The time when Foster sang of the Swany River no longer existed. When I had visited German's Rorela's Hill in 1989, I could not help but have a similar feeling.

Reverend Hwang was my friend who gave me hope and courage when I passed through the first phase of my ministry for the blind, and Reverend Hyung-Kil Kang is a friend who helped me greatly in specializing my ministry. He is currently the Senior Pastor of the True Way Church in Chicago, Illinois. He invited me to America several times and allowed me to receive rehabilitation training for the visually challenged, and he also helped me receive my Doctorate Degree in Ministry from McCormick Seminary.

Another partner I cannot forget is Reverend Jung-Il Lee who is currently serving at Kwang Jang Church in the city of Kwang Jang, below the town of Walker Hill in Seoul. For the last 20 years, he took interest in the visually handicapped ministry and has been helping me ever since he was at Young Nak Church. While he was serving at Young Nak Church, he created a Mother's Association and helped with the ministry for the blind. Since the time he has become a pastor at Kwang Jang Church, he continued his ties and cooperation with our Blind Evangelical Mission Organization.

About 10 years ago, a seminarian by the name of Jae-Hong Kim who had lost his sight when he was young, was brought to attend Kwang Jang Church by his wife. He had graduated with a business degree from Korea University, and was hired by The Bank of Korea. As he embarked on the journey of success, he lost his sight due to an eye infection.

Fortunately, they didn't have much difficulty in making a living because his wife was a graduate of the prestigious Ewha University and was working as a teacher. He was able to graduate from seminary with a scholarship provided by the Blind Evangelical Mission. After his graduation, he formed 'The Living Hope Mission Organization' which served and ministered to the blind people residing in Seoul.

Boasting a history of 10 years, The Living Hope Mission Organization is a unique organization that exists for those people whose blindness was caused by an accident. Kwang Jang Church actively supports the Blind Evangelical Mission and the ministries of the Living Hope Mission Organization.

Every Monday and Thursday, about 150 partially blind people gather together at the church for Bible study and Praise and Worship session, and for independent living. They learn to read and write braille, give massages, acupuncture, and finger pressure therapy. Their fervent prayers and will to become independent help with the church growth tremendously.

I am especially thankful to the woman's group who prepared church sponsored lunches every Mondays and Thursdays for the last ten years during these meetings for the partially blind. They even give their own money to prepare these lunches when the church is in financial trouble. Such volunteers are blessed and grow in their faith as they aid our blind sisters and brothers.

Today's churches hold many training programs for spiritual growth of its members. However, there are not that many volunteer programs to help our unfortunate neighbors. Kwang Jang Church is planning to make more service organizations to help many more visually disabled people.

The Story of Falling Into a Pit

I have a scar on my eye. Bicycles, pushcarts, open sewers, and lamp posts— such things give the visually handicapped much pain and suffering. As a visually disabled person, my forehead and knees receive the most blows. There probably isn't a single independent blind person who has not run into a lamp post or fallen into a ditch. My forehead and knees are full of scars. Especially on my lower right eye and eyelid, there remains a deep scar.

During my second year in seminary, I was residing in the living quarters at the seminary. I went out early Monday morning. There were no obstacles on the road in the morning, but coming back in the afternoon, something had been put up on the road. I was almost at the school when I heard shrieks of some students and an elderly lady behind me. I fell into a deep pit which had been dug up. My right eye and forehead were cut on a bag of shovels and pickaxes. My body was completely covered with dirt, and blood was flowing from my forehead and right eye. The situation was both embarrassing and awkward, not to mention painful. Although I was able to get out of the pit with some help, I soon lost consciousness.

When I awoke, a middle-aged lady who had witnessed the whole thing dusted the dirt off my clothes and took me to the hospital. I was taken to an eye hospital. I went through the emergency procedures and received nine stitches without anesthetics. Unbearable pain encompassed my body.

'Who in the world dug that hole in the ground!' Resentment and anger rose within me. Since it was the middle of the semester, the thought of missing school and receiving a lower grade made me even angrier. I asked my friend who always helped me, to find out who had dug the hole in the middle of the street. According to his investigation, it was a church across from the school. I told the hospital supervisor, and he told me to take the hospital bill to them. So I did.

Three days later, the senior pastor of the church visited me with one of the elders and the intern pastor. After worship, they told me the hospital bill would be paid by the church so I shouldn't worry. Having received their promise, my wound started to heal at an incredibly fast pace. However, I was worried about the scar. 'If there is a scar on my eyelid, it will hinder my ministry and give discomfort to others.' Such thoughts made me dizzy. God sent me to such a good school and helped me until now so He could use me as His servant. I was sure He would erase the scar. I stopped worrying. After six months, new flesh began to grow on the wound ; today, only a slight scar remains. Covered by my glasses and my eyebrow, the scar is barely noticeable.

I had no idea the church would become a leader in our ministry because of the wound I received there. Since my beloved friend became the senior pastor at the church, the church has become a role model in spiritually training partially blind people as well as giving them career training. Every year, due to accidents and diseases, 300 people lose their sight. This church is helping those who face difficult living conditions or are in despair because of their handicap to regain their independence and grow in faith.

Having lived for sixty some years, I have had my moments of sadness, thankful days, unfortunate days, happy days, and meaningful days. However, I feel that I had more painful and dangerous moments than others. Especially working for the visually handicapped, there are many unforgettable incidents. There were betrayals of trusted partners in the ministry and at times I have received undeserving criticism and scorn. All these have cultivated strength and wisdom in me so I could be who I am today.

Blessed Are Those Who Never Give Up

In February of 1986, we had opened the long-awaited Siloam Eye Hospital but there were no facilities necessary for performing surgery. To raise funds for the medical facilities, I left on a long journey to Toronto, Chicago and San Francisco. There was considerable difficulty catching a plane on my way to Toronto from New York. The apathy and lack of kindness on the part of the airline workers constantly made me feel uneasy. With no one to help me, I lost my luggage. At my wit's end, I grabbed a passerby and asked for help. Thankfully, he took me to the luggage claim area, but it was too late. Nothing was there.

Several hours later, utterly exhausted, I received word that my luggage was being kept at a certain hotel. My happiness and delight could not be expressed. As planned, I got on the plane from New York to Toronto and waited for takeoff. But unfortunately, because of heavy snowfall in Toronto, the flight was canceled. I waited all day and night in the airport. Once again, I got on the plane the next morning, but there still was too much snow in Toronto.

I didn't give up. I waited all day in the airport and boarded the plane again in the late afternoon. This time, the plane made it to Toronto. Ignoring my heavy fatigue, I arrived in Toronto and received a warm welcome from the members of the Blind Evangelical Mission. I had a wonderful time with them eating a dinner prepared with effort and loving care. When I requested funds for the needed equipment, they were happy to give them to me. Such a response brought me so much joy. All the weariness completely washed away the moment I heard their reply.

Unconditional Love

I was scheduled to go to Chicago after leaving Toronto. Many people greeted me with interest including my longtime friend. I lodged at his house and met many people. One woman told me that she read about the Siloam Eye Hospital in the newspaper and took great interest in our ministry. Over the course of our conversation, she promised to donate an OQ System which cost $40,000. This equipment was essential in eyesight recovery operations. I was so happy; I thought I must have been dreaming. That equipment is still in use, and I feel thankful whenever we use it.

I found out later that she did not have that kind of money. She had taken out a loan and spent the next two years paying it back. Later, she sent $30,000 to help build the Siloam House of Light behind the hospital. What a precious gift!

Ten years ago, to restore sight to our visually handicapped brothers and sisters, we held a charity concert in Chicago. Our crew left for Indiana around 11:00 pm and arrived at our destination at 4:30 in the morning. As we were about to unpack and get some sleep in the hotel, some pastors, deacons, and several people interested in our mission work knocked at our door, disturbing our sweet slumber. It was hard to get up again after such a short period of rest, but we had to move according to the schedule, which started at 7:00 in the morning and continued until 11:00 that night.

There are many people I would like to acknowledge for their help. I am confident that God will remember the names of such people who have blessed the Siloam Eye Hospital by opening their pockets and taking loans from banks without expecting any recognition or glory in return.

People Who Restore Light

For the last thirty years, I received help from partners and believers from all over the world. It is with their help I have come thus far.

One woman's last wish on her deathbed was to donate all her saving to be used for eye operations. Her daughter-in-law honored her last words, and brought the money to Siloam immediately following her mother-in-law's funeral. There was another instance where children collected an offering amongst themselves and gave it to Siloam as a tribute to their deceased mother. Another person sold his house and gave us all the proceeds. Immigrants in Toronto collected cans and sold them as well as placing donation boxes in stores, collecting coins. Through morning meetings, they raised funds and supported our ministry greatly over the last twenty years. Another eighty-year-old woman sold sesame oil to give light to one person a year. In another church, the entire congregation helped with a charity bazaar and gave all the proceeds as an offering.

There is yet another moving story I will never forget. A man who worked from 3:00 am until 11:00 in the morning as a street cleaner would collect boxes and iron scraps after work and sell them. All profits went to bring light to ten blind people in that particular year. What a beautiful act of love!

In another instance, a few fashion designers got together and held a bazaar for a week. The profits went to restoring the vision of hundreds of people that year. One company sent doctors to doctorless villages and sent enough funds to open 20 patients' eyes per month.

Because of such people giving away their love without expecting anything in return, 15,000 people have found light from darkness. But, there still remain many people in need of helping hands.

Pastors Who Helped
Without Recognition or Glory

Supplying Braille Bible and Hymnals

People with much love and warmth provide me with dreams, hopes, and unconditional love. I am convinced that I exist and work today because of their endearing love for me.

I go back 29 years and some of the faces I earnestly long to see surface in my mind. It was a time I had graduated from seminary and was working for a certain mission organization. Thinking it wasn't the right place for me, I decided to look for a place where I could broaden my influence of ministry.

Some of my close friends and I visited big city churches, but it was difficult then as it is now to find any satisfactory solutions. Almost all of the churches were very cold to us and told us that they already had their own programs. They flatly refused us. Despite the rejection, we prayed faithfully and knocked on many different doors.

I visited Reverend Sae-Jin Kim at Dongshin Church. I felt that Reverend Kim's heart was softening with every visit. My priority was getting braille Bibles and hymnals as the blind people flocked to our newly planted church for the blind. So I visited Reverend Sae-Jin Kim and explained everything to him.

He called Deacon Ki-Hwan Chang who was in charge of clerical matters, and told him, "Please send him away with 3 thousand won." Deacon Chang, who became an Elder since then, readily enclosed 3 thousand won in an envelope and sent me on my way. With that money, I purchased sixty Braille Hymnals.

That offering gave us the opportunity to obtain hymnals and start our worship service. As I endlessly visited one church after another, I happened to visit Dongshin Church once again. I had a meaningful conference with Reverend Jae-Chul Huh who was serving as the assistant pastor at that time.

Reverend Huh told me that for me to receive a continual support from Dongshin Church, I must persuade Reverend Sae-Jin Kim. Reverend Huh let me in on the tactic of winning Reverend Kim's heart. It was to visit often and bother Reverend Kim as much as possible. While I was practicing Reverend Huh's strategy on Reverend Kim, Reverend Ki-Won Han came in as the new pastor. It was time for Reverend Kim to retire. I had yet to jump over another hurdle.

The Establishment of a Support Organization for the Blind

One day when I visited Reverend Kim, I was told to discuss the matter over with the new pastor. Explaining our mission work to Reverend Han wasn't an easy task.

Even a hundred mile marathon starts with the first step. Following that example, I visited Reverend Han whenever I could and explained one thing at a time. Reverend Han understood quicker than I expected. He didn't rely on his power and authority, but he was easygoing and humble. In the midst of our conversation, if lunch time rolled around, he would order inexpensive noodles and share his lunch with me.

Finally, Reverend Han proposed we make up a formal support group for the visually handicapped. He said he would become the president of the organization to help me out so I should work hard. In 1976, the support group was formed, and in 1978, we held the Asia Mission Conference for the Blind. In 1981, Young Nak Church joined in the effort by holding a massive conference and concert at Saejong Cultural Center which literally rocked the city of Seoul. Of course it was to help the visually handicapped.

Dongshin Church also held a Christmas Banquet for the blind. That was when Reverend Kim was greatly moved by those with a visual handicap. The following New Year, he asked me to visit and gave me 200,000 won to use for my living expenses.

Reverend Kim helped me without praise or recognition for the next three to four years. But I have never used the money he gave me for my personal use. I spent it all on those brothers and sisters who needed it more than I. Both Reverend Kim and Reverend Han have passed away long ago. However, the love they demonstrated towards me shall remain in the deep recesses of my heart.

There is another individual I am thankful to. In 1970, to receive a visa and travel outside the country was more difficult than plucking a star from the sky. But with God's help, I was able to go to America, the country I had only dreamt about. The problem was the flight expense. A round trip cost about 50-60 thousand won which was a considerable sum of money at that time. It was impossible for me to produce that kind of money.

I prayed for wisdom. During my prayer, I was reminded of Supervisor Hyung-Nam Kim from my Junior High School years. He had always encouraged me to dream dreams and to have courage. He was the president and director of Soongsil University at the time. Whenever I visited him in difficult situations, he always gave me some allowances and showed me great generosity.

One morning, after the early morning prayer, I visited Professor Kim at his office. After paying him my respects with a deep bow, I sat down. Right away, he asked, "Reverend Kim, what do you need?"

I replied, "I am planning to visit America a week from now."

Then the Professor said, "You will be needing travel expenses."

After writing something down on a memo pad, he called one of the employees and told him to bring that amount. I was curious about the amount.

Without asking me about the flight tickets, he gave me 300,000 won. 300,000 won at that time is equivalent to US $4,000 today. I was so thankful and moved. I received that money and as soon as I came out of the office, I held onto the wall and shed uncontrollable tears as I prayed. Even after that, I visited him during holidays and paid him my respect. Without such precious individuals, I wouldn't exist today.

Soo-Chul,
I Will Live Your Share
of Life Too

One October Sunday in 1981, I met a visually handicapped boy who would give me a great shock later in life. His name was Soo-Chul Kim. In his second year of Junior High, he suffered a brain tumor and as a side effect, lost his eyesight. The bright and active boy had disappeared and in his black sunken eyes, only darkness remained. There was no one to comfort and give hope to such a boy.

Born in Pusan, his father was a professor at a university, and his brothers were smart students who went to the prestigious Seoul National University. Although he was born in a practically perfect family and environment, blindness came knocking at his door like a bad dream. After he lost his sight, he enrolled in Pusan Elementary School and learned to read and write braille. He learned to play the flute and played it whenever he felt frustrated and desperate. It comforted his heart. As he played, he became so good at it, he could pass for an amateur concert flutist.

One day, we had our dedication service for the Blind Evangelical Mission at a local church. We asked the music teacher at the school for a student who played well to participate in the service; the teacher introduced Soo-Chul to us.

As scheduled, immediately following the reverend's message, Soo-Chul started playing his flute. In the middle of his performance, he suddenly fell forward. Everyone was shocked; they carried him to the hospital right away. I felt extremely anxious. After the service, the reverend said, "Reverend Kim! Soo-Chul died. He was taken to Seoul University Hospital!" My heart sank with those words. How could this be? I grabbed a taxi and rushed to the hospital. When I arrived, he was already cold and stiff.

That night, Soo-Chul's brother and I were called into the police station for questioning. The next morning I went back to the hospital and crying endlessly as I stood there and thought it would have been better if my life had been cut short instead of his.

During the wake, I stood in front of Soo-Chul's coffin and promised him one thing. "I will learn the flute and play all that you couldn't. As I glorify God with my flute, I will always think of you. I'm sorry, Soo-Chul. You must be in our Father's embrace. I picture you in heaven where there are no tears, and no blindness."

We buried him at Yongin Cemetery. My feet were glued to the place in front of his tomb even after the burial was over. It felt like Soo-Chul was going to get up and follow me.

To keep my promise to Soo-Chul, I bought a flute with an honorarium I received. For a year, I practiced an hour every morning. I practiced until the building almost blew away. I practiced so hard that I would be playing the flute in my dreams. The very first piece I learned to play was "Amazing Grace".

After playing flute for the first time at a Wednesday night service, I gained courage. I just had to do it; so I learned. I practiced even more diligently. As I delivered messages at Korean-American Churches, I would play a hymn. I still have that flute in my office.

For there to be a Blind Evangelical Missions and a Siloam Eye Hospital, Soo Chul's death had to precede; sacrifice and mockery, ill-treatment and disbelief all had to be endured. There were those who hindered us rather than helping us, those who made us miserable, those who harshly attacked us thinking we were impure and unrighteous. But among them, there were martyrs and those who lived their entire life with the heart of a martyr. I think about Soo-Chul who became a sacrificial offering for the 200,000 blind and 5 million visually impaired people.

Soo-Chul! We will meet in heaven.

The Little Angels

In my mission work for the blind, I have experienced bone-shattering pain on more than one occasion. In spite of it all, I worked without looking after my body because I had my youth and faith.

To give a correct impression of the blind to local church pastors, I figured I needed some kind of opportunity. I contacted colleagues and decided to hold great revival meetings in metropolitan cities such as Pusan, Taegu, Pohang, and Kwangju to help the visually handicapped. It wasn't as easy as I thought. To accomplish a single revival meeting, I had to meet with each pastor at least two or three times, which cost me travel and lodging expenses.

We would take the 10:00 morning train to Pusan and arrive past 3:00 pm. We would dine in a restaurant and hold a meeting. By the time we confirmed our revival schedule and got back on the train, it would already be 11:00 pm. We would arrive back in Seoul at 6:00 the next morning. I would send the sisters who traveled with me back home and return to my office. In the office, I would wash up and start my day without getting any sleep. I would make the sisters who went with me come to the office by 1:00 in the afternoon. When we traveled, I would put them in first class since they were still young and I would take third class to lessen expenses. This continued for the next twenty years. We saved like ants to provide for eyesight recovery operations, scholarships, missions, and funds for the Church of the Blind.

In doing all this, I'm afraid I worked my little sisters too hard. Those who worked hard with me in the beginning have become wives and mothers. Some have become pastors' wives, others, wives of successful businessmen, and still others have become great housewives with children. We keep in frequent contact and spend time together as we talk about our memories of the past. The friendships and love born of Christ is truly rich and precious.

There are also singing angels at the Siloam Eye Hospital. We meet daily at morning chapel where we praise and worship before we start each day. A few minutes are dedicated to learning new praises and those with musical talent praise in the front.

As we gave praise in this manner, I discovered a few sisters from the nursing and administrative department who had beautiful voices. I picked out these few sisters and formed a choir. The choir became the 'Angel's Voice Choir'. We started a healing ministry by offering praise and worship time for the patients and guardians.

The choir practiced 30 minutes every day during lunch. They toured several churches and brought blessings upon the congregations through praise. The church choir conductors were full of amazement and compliments for our group. Although Angel's Voice wasn't made up of professionals, with much practice we were able to tour and glorify God through times of praise.

The choir also went overseas to Japan and to Korean-American churches in America to give testimonies and sing praises, Korean folk songs and children's songs to those who miss their homeland. Wherever we went, pastors and believers flooded us with love and welcomed us heartily. The singing angels contributed greatly in publicizing the Siloam Eye Hospital.

Life Stories

Although I Always Leave With Empty Hands...

Over the course of my ministry, I have visited Japan, America, Canada, Germany, Switzerland, and France broadening my ministry. It wasn't that I always had enough expenses to go. Although I felt desolate whenever I traveled without money in my pocket, I prayed throughout my journey as I held onto hope and entrusted everything to the Lord.

Sometimes I stayed for two, three and even six months. Staying in a foreign country meant spending large sums of money on lodgings, meals and many other travel expenses. It might be possible for a millionaire, but for a commoner like me, it truly is a difficult and burdensome situation. Despite it all, I left trusting God and expecting to receive warm love and care from my friends.

When I arrive at a destination, many friends come out to greet and welcome me as they guide me to my lodgings. Thankfully, when taking trips to America, quite a number of my colleagues invite me as a guest in their homes. I am thankful that I am welcomed by everyone wherever I go. Especially in New York, there are many places to stay because I have many colleagues there.

Wherever I go to deliver a sermon, I use the honorarium I receive to treat my fellow workers in Christ for lunch, pay them for their transportation services, gas and long distance phone bills. When I come back home after doing so, my joy is great. It is beautiful to give help and receive help. If you live generously, that generosity comes back to you, but if you live mercilessly, that mercilessness will also come back to you. I want to live a clean, greedless and selfless life. I am convinced that this must be the happiest life one could live. Because God knows I strive for that kind of life, God provides me with people who do the same.

How Can I Pay Back My Teachers' Goodness to Me?

To study with a visual disability among thousands of able students of was difficult beyond imagination. Such obstacles as studying without textbooks and the inability to read notes written on the blackboard come to mind as impossible factors. But because God gave me dreams and courage, what seemed impossible became possible for me. I owe it to my dedicated teachers who helped me and took precious care of me. How can I possibly pay back their goodness? I think leading a shameless life as a leader of the church and society might well be the greatest repayment I could offer.

Friendship That is Stronger Than Blood

My deep sentiment for friendships comes from such a desperate long-ing for them. I quietly reflect upon the loyalty and love of my friends over the last forty years. During my high school years when I had no house, I couldn't find lodgings from where I could easily attend school. I had a single room at a home for the visually disabled but there was the difficulty of having to transfer buses three times to reach my school. I had to get up at 4:00 and head out the door by 5:30.

It was so difficult for me that I had to find a room which was closer. A poor, blind boy was making a living by giving massages. I decided to move into his place. The new room I had moved to was a crowded place infested by bed bugs and fleas. The roof leaked when it rained and an open sewer ran three feet from the house. Running water was a rarity which prevented me from doing my laundry or washing myself frequently. Soon, I had lice clamoring all over my body. It truly was a pitiful sight. Skipping meals became the norm. While going through such hardship, a friend had helped me. He was the oldest son of an elder in a Methodist Church. Although he had to travel a long distance to get to school, he always came a little early and gave me the lunch he brought for himself. He sat next to me to read the blackboard for me or to find English vocabu-lary for me. He acted as my eyes regardless of where we were. He earned his tuition by doing private tutoring. After school, I followed him to the tutoring place. On his recommendation, they graciously offered me food and allowed me to lodge in their place with him. As we shared our joys and sorrows, we became closer than blood brothers.

During breaks, I would visit him and stay for weeks on end. The tasty meals his mother used to make — steaming potatoes and corn, wheat flour dumplings – are all still so very vivid in my memory. He was a friend who truly applied the words of Jesus, "Love each other as I have loved you. Greater love has no one than this, that he lay down his life for his friends"(John 15:12~13).

Grandmother Sung-Rae Chung

I am reminded of an elderly lady who came to see me in the middle of the night. A Few years ago, I had an opportunity to speak at a one-day revival meeting at Tokyo Church which boasted a long history and tradition.

The weather was very cold that day, and the snow had fallen to ankle depth. Japan's cold weather was much harsher than Korea's. After the Sunday message, I slept in a room which the Senior Pastor Reverend Kun-Shik Kim provided for me. At 5:30 in the morning, I came outside to head toward the airport for my flight.

But an elderly lady, Sung-Rae Chung was waiting for me outside the church. Surprised, I asked her what had brought her here on a cold snowy night. She answered that she was so blessed by my message last Sunday that she wanted me to pray for her before I left and deliver a small offering enough for one person to have an eye sight restoration operation. For those two reasons, she came by the 4 o'clock train, the earliest train of the day, and waited outside 30 minutes in the cold.

I was so touched by her love and concern, I could not hide my tears. She came to Japan at an early age and went through all kinds of hardships. She wasn't a wealthy lady at all. She made a meager living by renting out a few rooms of her shabby old house, but she served the church faithfully and treated pastors well whenever they visited her house.

This elderly lady who came by the 4 am train and waited for me under the falling snow to restore light to a single visually disabled person. Whenever I go back to Japan, she never sends me back empty handed. She manages to give me what little she had saved over the period of a year or so.

Because such people exist, we can restore the light of love to our neighbors. There are millions of people on this earth who are far wealthier than her! The church being the Body of Christ of love, must give to those who do not have the power to repay. I send my gratitude from the depth of my heart once again to that angel-like grandma who waited a long time in the snow.

My Disciple Who Acted as My Eyes for a Year and a Half

Since my high school years until the end of my college years, I served as a teacher at Sunday School. And during my seminary years, I was in charge of the Elementary, Junior High and Young Adult Group as a pastor intern. That is why many former students greet and help me wherever I go. Out of the numerous disciples, a few of them are simply unforgettable.

It was a time when I was a Education pastor intern at a certain church in Su-Yu-Ri. At the time I was hired, there were 40-50 students in the Elementary Ministry and 20-30 in the Youth Group. The senior pastor told me to make sure I increased the number any way I knew how.

Prayer, the Word of God, and visitations were required necessities in order to bring a revival to the church. However, it was very difficult for me to go on visitations. I was receiving inadequate payment from the church, and with my wife's pregnancy, we had many problems. The church didn't even provide me with transportation fees or a church fund for fellowship.

But God opened a door for me. There was a student who had just come up from Hwang Deung which was in the northern part of Cholla Province with his parents. He was taking a year off in order to get into high school. So I asked him to study in the morning and evening, and help me during the day for a year. I asked him to go on visits with me, read me books and be my eyes. He readily agreed.

It took three bus stops to get to the church from our house. Time wise, it was a 30-40 minute trip. My little helper was always prompt in guiding me to the church and consistently helped me with the visitations. I recommended him to my alma mater, Soongsil High School. He applied and was accepted.

I had developed a close relationship with him, and I met with him often after resigning from that church. I also made it a point to always keep him in my prayers. He was a very talented vocalist. I suggested that he go to a music school. After graduating from high school, he pierced through the tremendous competition and entered into Seoul National University School of Music. Currently, he is a Music teacher at his former high school, and he also glorifies God as a Choir Director. I taught three of his brothers, and his parents also liked me very much.

As it is in the old saying, if you mistreat a disabled person, you will be punished but if you love him, you will be blessed. God could only have blessed him because he sacrificed a year and a half to look after a blind person like me. I thank God who made me realize through my beloved student that if one serves the weak for God's glory, he will be guaranteed a heavenly reward.

Overcoming Death Three Times

There have been many times I was faced with death. While I can't record all the times the love of God has protected me against death, I would like to mention three incidents.

In the autumn of the year the war broke out, I was assigned the task of putting old cotton batches into the willowing machine, and, when it came out, I would soften it up by stepping on it. The finished batch of cotton was put into a basket. One day, a chicken came along and soiled the finished cotton with its droppings. When my aunt found out, she mercilessly threw a hard wooden pillow at me as she shouted, "Keel over and die!" The wooden pillow hit me on the nose and lips squarely. My nose became a floodgate of blood and my tooth was chipped. My nosebleed was so bad, it seemed like someone had turned on the faucet but forgot to turn it off. Right then, a middle-aged man was passing by and, seeing me, asked if he could rest in the house for a while. He blocked the nosebleed with cotton balls, flipped my head back, and gently jabbed my back with his fist. Not having witnessed the scene where the wooden pillow was thrown at me, he asked what had happened. My aunt was ready with a lie. "This boy cannot see where he is going, so he ran into the pillar as he was coming out of the room by himself." I was flabbergasted. The nosebleed stopped, but I still had a busted lip and chipped tooth. Likewise, there is not a single unharmed part in my body. God healed me when my eardrums were impaired due to cruel beatings I received. God straightened my broken nose caused in much the same way.

There was another instance of a close encounter with death. A friend who lived in New York was suffering from bone marrow cancer. After many years fighting cancer, he finally had to have his leg amputated. I thought about how uncomfortable it must be to have a leg amputated. I felt horrible about the whole situation.

Around that time, I had an opportunity to visit Los Angeles. Upon my arrival in LA, I called him and offered words of consolation. He was glad to hear from me and suggested we get together for a few days. He told me to cancel my plans and rush to New York. I reserved a flight. Two days later, I received a call telling me to hasten my return to Korea. I had to give my report to my church denomination. Having no time to lose, I called my friend and told him my situation. I promised to visit him during Thanksgiving. Two weeks after I returned home, I heard the broadcast that a Korean plane had crashed in Russia. That very plane was the one I had reserved to come back on from New York. If I had visited my friend at that time, I would have died.

After that, there followed the third near death situation. We invited a famous vocalist Professor Hyun-Myung Oh for a 'Siloam Charity Concert to raise funds for the eyesight recovery operations'. We toured through Washington, Chicago, and Atlanta. After the concert, Professor Oh went to Germany, and Elder Woon-Kook Yang and our team were to arrive in Korea via L.A. But right after the plane took off, the whole plane was quickly filled with smoke, and the flight attendants were moving about busily. When asked if something was wrong, they all replied that absolutely nothing was the matter. Thirty minutes later, we received a message from the pilot through the speakers.

"There has been an engine failure. The most important engine number 3 has given out. We have replaced the third engine with the fourth, however, we cannot go to our destination but we have to lay over in Anchorage, Alaska. We ask for your kind understanding." The airplane was shaking violently and the air was filled with smoke. The three hundred passengers almost suffocated in the smoke. I meditated on Psalm 23 and prayed.

"God, help me. I still have so much to do for the visually disabled. If you end my life here and now, you are the one who's missing out, Lord." The plane finally had an unstable landing at Anchorage Airport. Everyone was amazed when they got off and saw that one of the engines had been completely destroyed. The thought that we had been so close to death made all of us shudder. I said this right then and there: "I am a pastor. I prayed for a safe landing. God helped us."

The passengers sat themselves down on the floor and benches of Anchorage airport. The manager of the airport came to let us know that he would be first taking the passengers with children, disabilities and the elderly to the hotel. The rest would stay and receive a tour of the area. But that was a lie. They first took the passengers from the first and second class; the passengers with children, and disabilities or the elderly were obviously being neglected for an indefinite period of time.

Elder Woon-Kook Yang who was traveling with me at the time finally demanded to be helped. It was only then they came to our aid. We arrived at the hotel at a very late hour of the night, giving us only four hours of sleep before the morning takeoff. Thinking back on that incident sends a chill down my spine even now. But I give glory to God that He had let me live.

The Story of a Flight Attendant on a Plane to Atlanta

I remember an unforgettable tale that happened to me five years ago. In order to raise funds for the eye operations, I had to travel to Atlanta via New York. After staying with my friend for a few days, he took me to Kennedy Airport to board a plane headed to Atlanta. The airport was so crowded that day that parking was next to impossible. My friend had no choice but just to drop me off at the entrance. Before he took off, he asked the airline staff to help me with all the boarding procedures including the boarding itself.

I sat down in my seat guided by the flight attendant. The attendant was exceptionally tall and beautiful. She even buckled my seat belt for me, and explained about the emergency exit in explicit detail. She told me that she would personally be responsible for my safety and comfort during this trip to Atlanta. Once the plane took off, that same attendant came to me and asked this and that about myself. Where did I come from, what I did for living, how I had lost my eyesight, etc. I answered every one of her questions truthfully and honestly.

She told me that her husband was a pastor of a Baptist church, and that he had fought in the Korean War. Although she used to be a Quaker, she changed her religion upon marrying her husband. She gave me more snacks than other passengers. She even spread cheese on my bread so that it was easier for me to eat. When we arrived at Atlanta, she led me out the exit before any other passenger.

Atlanta's airport is more crowded than other airports. Therefore, it is really easy to get lost if you don't pay attention. I rode the shuttle train for about ten minutes right after getting off the train to reach the exit. The plane was scheduled to take off to another place that night. There wasn't much time until the take off.

Reverend Jung-Do Park who was to meet me at the airport had not arrived yet. The attendant had to go back to the airport and we were getting worried. To comfort me, she said, "Since I'm the head flight attendant on that plane, they can't leave until I get back on." Then she started to sing a praise song.

"God sent his Son, His name was Jesus..." I sang along with her. I told her that my friend was going to come for sure and that she should get back to her work. But she kindly insisted that, "it is my responsibility to protect and help Reverend Sun-Tae Kim from Korea. Helping you will please God the most." When my friend showed up 30 minutes late, it was rather she who said to me, "thank you for waiting." I got her address and sent her a pretty blouse when I got back to Korea.

Escape From A War Camp

This story goes all the way back to my begging days. One day, a jeep came out from the military base and the driver told me to get in. Sitting in the jeep were the army chaplain and driver. He said "Good morning" as he warmly shook my hand. We drove about twenty minutes from the base until we arrived at a small house. It was a home for seriously wounded soldiers receiving treatment. There were about a 100 patients in near fatal condition, screaming constantly throughout the night. It was a horrifying place to be. There were patients without arms, those who had lost their sight, others almost dying from severe wounds, those who had their legs amputated, people without hands, soldiers shot in the waist, etc. Most of them had to be hand fed, but those capable of eating on their own would quickly finish their food and try to steal from the others. This created fights and arguments during mealtime.

I was one of the most able-bodied among them. Because I could talk, walk, and had both arms, I could move around more freely than them. Since they only gave us breakfast and dinner, I had to substitute a glass of milk for lunch. I felt like I was in a tiger's hole. I thought that a life of beggary would be better than this. If I was caught trying to run away, I would nearly be killed by harsh punishment. While I tried to come up with a good plan, I met an elderly couple that came to visit their wounded son. I told them my situation. They told the guard that they wanted to take me out to buy me some bread and lunch, so the guard let us go.

I went to the train station and started to beg for help of others. If I went back to the military base, I was afraid of running into the same chaplain. I was afraid of being sent back to the war camp. I decided to go far away from both places. I moved to the East Gate and spent much of my remaining begging years there.

Giving to God all the Unfair Treatment I Had Received

There are times in a person's life when one just wants to let out screams and cries of anger and bitterness at the unfair treatment one has received. One has only revenge in mind. I believe I am one of those people who have received such treatments more than anyone else.

Upon graduating from seminary, I started a church for the blind. My life then was very dismal and dark. I had a wife, a little daughter, and my in-laws living in a single room. I was often anxious about what we should eat. I started to tutor English privately or taught English conversation to a group of nurses interested in going to America. I was able to earn living expenses and my transportation fees in that way.

While I was involved with such affairs, I was introduced to an English missionary. I was to help with his work and in return, he paid me 40,000 won a month. It was precious money to me. Since the mother of the missionary also had a visual disability, she took great interest in Korea's visually disabled. For several months, the missionary and I discussed everything day and night like real brothers.

Around that time, a Korean man who had married an English woman was hired as the director. Although he had only accepted Christ a year before, he tried hard to exceed the pastor in every way. I took it as a thorn God had given me and persevered through it with faith. I fought against the anger and bitterness I felt from such unfair treatment. However, it was hard to face the humiliation and betrayal.

I had an errand boy working under me. His pay was a 10,000 won more than mine. I asked the director why the errand boy was getting a better pay than I was when I was older and had better education. He replied, "It's because he can see and you can't." I was angry enough to gouge out his eyes had Christ not been in my heart.

I can't express the anger I felt. Other visually disabled people were applying to the same company. They reasoned I didn't really know the world of the visually disabled because I went to a regular school and never had to learn braille. Later, I found out a woman secretly stole from me and was being paid for my work.

I reached one truth while I experienced such unrighteous acts against me. Not all people are human; you are only human if you treat others with a humane heart. I decided I had nothing more to learn at that place. Not only that, I believed receiving such ill treatment and humiliation would cause serious damage to my life, so I decided to move on. Once I decided to go, my heart calmed down like a serene sea.

The verse that reads, "Revenge is the Lord's; therefore, do not repay evil with evil but repay it with good" is the truth. When in our lives, we face unfair treatment that causes our heart to be bitter and angry, we need to bring it before the Lord who takes care of all things.

Thief!

There are times you leave your wallet in the bus or your house is robbed. I have twice entertained unwelcome night guests in my life.

During my college years, I moved into a room my friend had rented. Since graduation was drawing near, and I couldn't stay in the dorm any longer, and I moved everything into his place. I had finally put an end to my four years of dorm life. My friend's room was located in a ghetto. The room was built with clay bricks so that water dripped onto the bookshelves and blankets whenever it rained. There were three of us living together. One would get water from the well, the other would cook, and I would peel potatoes and do the dishes after the meal.

One cold winter night, one of the friends screamed, "Thief!" The night guest was so surprised he ran away, picked up some weights and threw them at us. The weight fell next to my ears. Had it hit me directly, I could have died. It was a dangerous moment indeed. The thief that came into our house that night was caught after some time. The shock was great when we discovered that he was a resident of our town who dropped by our church from time to time.

A few years later after I had married, my family settled down in a run down shack. The house was given to me free by one of the missionaries when I worked for a mission agency. Because it was such an old house, it was infested with fleas, bed bugs and mice. The smell of the briquette gas from the house across the street along with the reeking smell of the bathroom pierced our noses. The door was only for show; it was non-functioning. We lived in that house for about five years. Trusting in God's protection, we sometimes had to leave our children in that house unattended. One day we visited one of my friend's house who had several puppies. We picked out the cutest one and brought it home with us. It didn't take long to see that it was a smart dog.

One cold winter night, the crazy yelping of the puppy woke me up. He was scratching at my door and making a funny noise. Being suspicious, my wife looked out the door. There was a dark figure standing in our yard. My wife was white with fear. After calming her down, I went outside, bowed politely and earnestly to our night guest. "How tired you must be at this time of the night? I am a pastor who spreads God's Word. Please come into our room. We will warm up the soup and serve you a nice, hot meal. I don't have much money, but I can provide you with some clothes or traveling expenses. I will not call the police. And besides, I'm blind."

After listening to all that I had to say, the thief said, "I'm sorry. I understand. I will just be on my way," and with that, he went away.

The Thief Who Regained His Conscience

Afraid that a thief might break in again at any time, I had a hard time falling asleep at night after that incident. But moving wasn't such an easy task. However, an amazing thing happened.

I had to walk to a bridge about ten minutes away in order to get on the bus. One day, as I was crossing the bridge after getting off work, someone tapped me on the shoulder. "Excuse me," he said. "I'm the thief that broke into your house the other day. I was deeply moved by what you said to me that night. I changed my mind to work hard for a living. I started a little business selling roasted silk worms. I even started to attend church. I'll go visit you once I earn a lot of money."

It was truly an amazing encounter. In Proverbs, it is said that if you treat an evil person with humble and soft words, you will preserve your life. If I had screamed "Thief!" that night, he might have harmed us with the weapon he had brought. Because I treated him with love, I was able to bear beautiful fruit.

The Sacrificial Love of Siloam Mothers

Friends who cry with you, feel hurt with you, share your sorrow when you are hungry, and comfort you in times of misery are truly beautiful and precious friends. But this world does not operate on such principles. The world has more people who make those who are already miserable even more miserable, and lead those people who are in despair into deeper despair.

But even among them, I would like to introduce some beautiful mothers. There was a place called "Yang Dong" in front of the Seoul Train Station during the 1960-1970's. The place was comparable to Sodom and Gomorra. The government scattered the unethical people who were living in that area into the outskirts of the town. That left some empty houses in that area and soon, they were occupied by poor brothers and sisters and visually disabled people.

They made a living by begging, or selling pens or chewing gum as they sang on trains, buses, restaurants, or cafes. With their daily earnings, they paid rent and survived on the leftovers. Living like that left no hope for them. They just had to learn to be content with the reality of their mundane life.

There were also many of them who considered alcohol their one and only pleasure in life. And there were also those who cooked rice and boiled water on a tiny furnace they had in the room.

Under such unfortunate conditions, a tragedy took place. A visually disabled couple had a baby. When the baby was only a year old, the mother accidentally poured boiling water on the baby. The baby died on the spot. I was so heartbroken when I heard the story.

I thought about how I could comfort them and give them new hope . I made some calls to those who also wanted to help and brought the unfortunate couple rice cakes and canes. But those contributions could not give true comfort or get to the root of their problems.

I finally asked the Siloam Mother's Group in the region of Yang Dong to help the visually disabled brothers and sisters in that area. They readily agreed as they thought such things were their rightful duty. They soon went over there and started to do the laundry for the visually disabled in Yang Dong as well as distribute rice to them.

The Ye Neung Church for the blind was also planted right around that time. The visually disabled residents of Yang Dong started to attend the church one by one. The foundation of Ye Neung Church was slowly being built up by those visually disabled brothers and sisters of Yang Dong. They started to join the choir and attend the young adult meetings. They began to change. The Siloam Mother's Group kept up with the change, helping them every way they could.

Light illuminated from the faces of once hopeless ones as they boasted of experiencing a heartwarming mother's love and of having received humane treatment. With the help of the government, the visually disabled residents of Yang Dong were moved to a rehabilitation center operated by the Catholic Church. Those same people built Canaan Church there and became the leaders of the church. The Yang Dong area has now turned into a major business district with the Hilton Hotel and the Daewoo Building lining the streets.

The prayers, concerns, and love of the Siloam mothers played a major role in opening up a new page in the lives of those who had once lost hope. What a thankful story! I would like to deeply thank the sacrificial love of the Siloam Mothers.

Mother of Faith who Treated Me Like a Part of the Family

When I look back on my past, I can be assured of God's presence in every step of the way. I received much love from many people—so much love that I can't even repay it with my life. I especially cannot forget the love I received from Mothers of the faith.

Forty-five years ago, I had ended my long career as a beggar and had finished everything needed to enter junior high school. The orphanage I lived in served us horrible food. Sometimes, we had rice, and at other times we would eat fried batter made of rotten corn powder as the main meal of the day. There were days when we couldn't even get that and had to starve the whole day.

Some neighbors took the opportunity to sell rotten dried bread to the orphans. They told the orphans that they could pay them back at a later time. Not knowing they were rotten, the orphans would purchase it and eat it under a blanket so that they wouldn't have to share it with anyone.

During this time, one woman poured out kindness and grace to me. She had left her husband in North Korea, and took refuge in the South. She lived with a son and a daughter and sold rice cakes in the fish market. She sometimes sent over a plate of bean-fried cakes through her daughter. Other times, she even sent over maki, fried cakes, and glutinous-rice cakes. She somehow managed to afford to get a calf and made me a veal cuisine when I was nothing but bones because of malnutrition. She didn't even give such things to her own children.

220

My high school years were truly rough. There was no way of expressing my misery and loneliness at not having any money, a home, parents or relatives. On top of that, to study among a couple thousand able students of non-disability was difficult. My only wish at that time was to live near the school so I didn't have to ride the bus back and forth. I prayed about it for a long time. One day, a deacon from the Freedom Church told me to come live at her place with her kids and study with them.

Her house was located on a hill right next to the high school. Although her husband was a nonbeliever, he was a good man who never opposed his children attending church. With their two sons and four daughters, they lived in a three-bedroom house. It wasn't a big house by any means. Having no running water, they had to carry water all the way back from the hill at Soodo Girl's High School. But if it didn't rain for a while, it was even more difficult to get a bucket of water. In spite of it all, she took me in and treated me like part of the family so that I could attend my junior and high school comfortably.

I would also like to introduce another person who had been a great help to me. The Siloam family prayed every morning for over ten years during the morning prayer hour for the "House of Light" to be built next to the hospital on the piece of land we had purchased from elder Chang-Keun Choi.

I also went from place to place trying to find people who would help us and although the Siloam staff gave an offering from time to time for this purpose, we didn't even come close to being able to start the project.

Then one day, the president of Kyung Won Theater came to us with an offering. I was shocked by the amount. He was the type of person who wouldn't even waste a single grain of rice. But God answered our eleven years of prayer through him. With that as our foundation, we were encouraged to start the building project for the "House of Light." We were, however, still short on money.

All I could do was to depend on God in prayer. Soon, Elderess Bang-Hee Eun and Elderess Kwi-Ja Kim along with many others started to raise more funds for the project. They brought in more support than I could have ever imagined.

The idea of building the Light House was inspired and made possible by the little seed that was planted by Elderess Choong-Sup Yoon's family. Not only her family, but there are many people of different age groups and social status who visited our Siloam Eye Hospital. The young adults treated me like their real brother or family as we shared in love and fellowship. The elderly are like my mother and father in Faith. They treat me warmly and give offerings. It is because of their hidden service and love that I can exist today.

How can I ever pay back the debt of love I owe them? I would like to repay them by dedicating my body, soul and mind to serving my poor neighbors. As long as there is breath in me, I shall always cherish and remember their love.

When I Am Weak, God is Strong

All people have both strengths and weaknesses. It is only natural for someone with good eyes to have a bad sense of smell, or good hearing to have a weak throat, or strong stomach to have bad kidneys.

More than eighty percent of my body is weak. As I have said several times already, my body is full of weaknesses from being beaten, sleeping on cold floors, and getting soaked in the rain without clothes to change into. My head is stained with many scars.

Although the scars from being beaten by rods when I was little have healed, I still have severe migraines from having bled so much. Because I have been slapped so many times, my eardrums have suffered damage. They have healed since, but both ears sometimes go numb and painful.

The pain in my eyes is also severe, because I could not receive treatment at the time of my accident. My wounded eyes were left to heal themselves. This caused my eyes to deteriorate and cataracts came creeping in. Just as even the best dishes tarnish with rare usage, eyes form cataracts when they are not put to use for a long period.

But the most important part of my body which gives me much pain is my back. Because I have slept in cold places on winter nights, been kicked by people in my side, and hit with clubs by my relatives, you can hear the bones cracking from my back when you touch it. The pain that comes from sitting still in one spot for a long time is unbearable. I also have major rheumatism in my shoulders and arms.

In my childhood years, when I was lonely, in pain and sick, I had prayed to God, "If you let me live, I will live righteously and show love towards people like myself." Because I had prayed that prayer and promised God to live a good life, I do not want to live with bitterness in my heart. I want to give everything I have and serve others. There have been many times when people have taken advantage of my good intentions and motives.

The Apostle Paul said that even though he had many things to boast about, he would boast of his weaknesses instead. It is because God's amazing power manifests itself through our weaknesses.

There is an American saying that the early bird gets the worm. There is a similar saying in Korea: "If you open your front door and clean up early in the morning, many blessings will come to you." Both of these insinuate that God will help you if you live a diligent and faithful life. Living a diligent and faithful life will prevent you from losing out.

I gained this experience as a beggar in my childhood years. If you go to restaurants or private residents early in the morning, you get a bucket full of rice and side dishes. However, if you wake up late, you will have to satisfy yourself with the leftovers.

I believed that God would bless me if I lived a faithful life. Because I had learned to live a diligent life since I was small, I try my best to live more diligently than anyone else.

I start my day at 3:40 in prayer and meditation on the Word of God. I arrive at the Siloam Eye Hospital by 6:10 am, and through the speaker system, I send out a message and prayer. Then, I go around visiting each patient one at a time, giving them hope and courage through the love of

Christ. I return home around 8:00 or 9:00 in the evening. The rest of my time is spent preparing the message for the next day. I have done this for the last 25 years.

I don't know how much longer God will grant me life on this earth. But until the day I die and as long as my health permits, I would like to visit lonely people with visual disabilities to spread God's Word of comfort to them, pray with them, treat them to delicious food, and freely give them what they need. I don't want any prestige or greed in my life. I simply want to give my life to the work I have been given.

Joyous Pains

The Banana Incident

There are times when you experience sweet tragedies and joyous pains as you live your life. I have discovered through experience that joyous pains are those difficult times which change into joy and meaningfulness in the days to come.

Our country was suffering economically during the 70's through 80's. These days, you can purchase a bundle of bananas at 2 to 3 thousand won(about two dollars). But back then, not only were they rarely seen, it cost 10,000 won for just one banana.

During the early 80's I was able to buy all the bananas I ever wanted in Japan. I bought 30 bananas from Japan and returned to Korea. The airport inspections were very strict at that time. The inspectors would turn the luggage of passengers completely upside down, looking through every single item. The only present I had on me were the bananas. Thankfully, the inspector was a member of the New Visitation Church and therefore let me pass without giving me a hard time.

I was planning to give the bananas to a reverend I had great respect for, but I was worried to take the bananas home. My two daughters were quite young back then. The oldest one was six and the second one was four. We couldn't even provide them with snacks at that time. If I took the bananas home, they would inevitably want to have some. I didn't know what I could do if they asked for them.

The pastor of Pusan's Sojung Church had allowed us to use their facility to hold a night of dedication service when our mission work was very precarious. Because of that single dedication service, we were able to raise enough moneys to last us a year. I was encouraged by that experience. I discovered the truth that I could do all things through Christ who gives me strength.

Just as I had expected, as soon as got through the door, my daughters looked through my things and asked me immediately, "Daddy, can we have some bananas?"

I told them, "Kids, those are for the pastor in Pusan. I'll buy you lots of them next time I go to Japan." In this way, I tried to pacify them. My two daughters probably wanted them badly, but they obeyed me and never asked for them again.

The next day, I took the train to Pusan with the bananas in one hand and rice cakes in the other. I delivered the present into the hands of the pastor's daughter and came right back to Seoul.

I fell into a deep thought on the return train. 'If I had bought one more bunch of bananas and given it to my girls, how they would have enjoyed eating them!' When I think about how much my little daughters must have wanted to eat those bananas, my heart still aches to this day. But the only way to adequately thank the Sojung Church pastor was to present him with the bananas I had.

After that, the Sojung Church dedicates at least one week a year as the week for the Visually Disabled. They help us with more offerings and prayers than any other church. The Sojung Church's Pastor also became my father in faith, and I have fellowship with his family as if they were my own.

The Unforgettable Life in the Orphanage

In a short period, I experienced six different orphanages. Some orphanages only provided breakfast and dinner, and some orphanages couldn't even do that. For example, they would plop a tin can filled with wheat rice on the table. The orphans would sit around the table and each take a ball of rice from the can. The only side dish we would get was salt. Sometimes, when scraps of beef happened to be in the soup, the kids would scream, "It's beef soup!" At other times, when canned fish came out, the kids' screams with ecstasy, "It's meat!"

The tragedy of my insignificant life all began with such days. Whenever beef soup or canned fish appeared on the table, the big orphans approached the little ones and said, "I'll give you candies, and chocolates, bread and crackers the American soldiers give me if you will surrender your meat to me now." And the little ones had no choice but to hand over their meat to the older bullies.

Sometimes, when flour dumpling stew with strips of beef would come out, the bullies again would talk the little ones into giving them up for a false promise of something grander. "If you give me half of your stew today, I'll give you my white rice when it comes out next time." In hopes of eating more white rice, the innocent little orphans would sacrifice their food that day for a promise of a better day. I wasn't an exception. I too, was deceived several times by their sweet lies.

But such false deals always brought about misbehavior on the part of those who had gotten their food taken away. Those who had to surrender their meal inevitably felt the unbearable hunger pangs in the middle of the night. This led them to secretly sneak into the kitchen and steal food from the rice pot. One night, two of my roommates tempted me to go steal food from the kitchen. I was so hungry that night, I consented to go with them.

Upon opening the rice pot, we discovered several bowls of rice. They were meant for the night shift staff. One of my friends handed me a bowl to eat. We had to pass through a long hallway in order to reach our room. I believe the distance was about 200 meters from our room to the kitchen. We were walking on our tiptoes, trying our hardest to not make a sound. But a few feet away from us stood Teacher Suk, the disciplinarian of the orphanage. I knew he favored me. However, just one wrong move, and he would beat you with a club until you've tasted death. Everyone in the orphanage feared him.

We all thought, "We are so dead." Fortunately, the light wasn't on so the hallway was still dark. I unbuttoned my shirt and stuffed my bowl of rice under my armpit, then walked toward him as if nothing was the matter. For some unknown reason, Teacher Suk spoke softly to us as he passed by, "Where are you guys coming from at this time of the hour? Go into your room and go to sleep." My friends and I let out a sigh of relief at having our lives spared. We sat underneath an old tree and finished our rice.

No matter how many times I think about it, there was no way Teacher Suk could have missed the rice bowls in our hands. My friends told me that since Teacher Suk favored me, he pretended not to have seen. But as I think about it now, I come to realize God had blinded Teacher Suk's eyes out of His love for me. Reflecting back to my orphanage years, I promise myself to live a sinless life without regrets.

Even the Barking of a Dog Can Sound Like the Voice of an Angel

I remember an episode that happened deep in the woods one cold winter night. The sun had gone down and the weather was getting colder and colder. After going from one house to another begging for food, I asked if they would allow me to stay overnight at their place. I wasn't asking for a nice bedroom, I was only asking for any old corner I could rest my tired body. Although they gave me food, not a single house agreed to let me stay.

At a certain house, an elderly man came out. He told me that not far from there was a little town where there were resting places and guest rooms that were open to anybody free of charge. I had no choice but to go in search of that place, groping about in complete darkness. The way to that town was rough and jagged. I think I crossed high mountains and deep and wide streams. From deep in the woods came the howling of wild night creatures and the cold winter wind that blew mercilessly seemed to cut through my body. Carrying the big staff the elderly man gave me, I successfully crossed the stream. There was still no sign of a town.

After traveling some more, I faintly heard the barking of a dog. Thinking that it must be a sign of a town, I whistled aloud and screamed into the air. I figured that if the dog heard my whistling and barked more that would be a sure sign that I was closer to the town. The more I walked, the more clearly I heard dogs barking. Soon, I heard the rambunctious noises of the dogs. They were coming from all directions. One dog's barking had set off the others.

'I'm okay now. I'll live after all.' Having gathered courage and strength, I headed toward the town. The town came closer and I felt like the dogs were barking right in front of me. Thinking the dogs were barking at the front entrance of some house, I headed that direction.

"Hello! Somebody help me! I'm dying here!"

No one answered my call. The dog kept barking. I didn't know what to do other than go around the town and look for something—anything.

From somewhere, I heard the sound of people droning in the night. 'Now I'm safe. I'll be okay' I said to myself. I went over to the sound of the voices. I asked for help in a very loud voice, "Please help me. I'm a beggar boy. I have no where to sleep so I'm wandering around like this in the middle of the night."

That was the very guest house the old man had told me about. All the elderly men of the town were gathered there playing a game of *yut* and enjoying acorn-starch jelly as their night snack. An old man opened the door and asked me, "Who are you? Why are you traveling at night? Where did you come from?" To his questions, I gave a detailed introduction of myself.

"Please let me sleep here for the night. I'm not the kind that will steal anything. I can't even see."

One of the old men listened carefully and told me to come in. He gave me a bowl of acorn-starch jelly. After talking to me and asking me several questions, he said, "You are a smart kid. How did you lose your eyesight?" I told him my life story up to that point.

A very elderly man told me, "You leave good a impression. I can even see some wealth in your face. You will definitely live well in the future. You will become a great hero someday." He told me my fortune by doing a little face-reading. The night deepened as I talked with them. One by one, they returned to their homes and I was left to sleep alone in the warm and cozy guest room.

The next morning, the house owner kindly gave me some warm water to wash my face and feet. Not having washed myself in a very long time, I felt like I was truly alive. He even treated me to hot radish soup with white rice and Kimchi. I received a pair of warm socks along with a set of clothes. On my way out, he repeatedly told me to be careful.

The reason I could sleep in a country guest house in that cold winter night was all due to the barking of the dogs. Their barking gave me the hope that a town was nearby and that hope kept me from freezing to death. Sometimes, even the barking of the dogs can sound as precious as the voices of the angels. Many times, we use a dog's name in vain. But dogs let the owner know if the thief is in the house, or sometimes, they play the beautiful role of angels, leading a lost boy like me to town.

What is the Most Fearful Thing in the World?

People will give all kind of answers to the question "What is the most fearful thing in the world?" Some will say fire. If a house is on fire, people, possessions and everything will be burned to ashes. And others might say water. If there is a flood, the house and everything inside will drift away. And still others might say a thief. A thief can take everything and in the end can harm your life.

There might also be people who will say passing by the cemetery at night. Many dead people are in their tombs and sometimes phosphorous lights flicker from the tombs, scaring the passersby. But according to my experience, a cemetery isn't a scary place at all. During my childhood begging days, several beggar companions and I slept most of our summer nights in the cemetery, using tombs as our pillows. During the day, we would sit on the rock table made for ancestor worship and play all day long. We would eat chestnuts from the nearby chestnut trees and enjoy eating fruits off the lime tree. Even now, if asked whether I can walk in front of the cemetery by myself at night, I would answer with an affirmative yes without a moment of hesitation.

If someone asked me what the most fearful thing in the world is, I would answer, "people." This is the lesson I have learned throughout my life. I have seen a mother and baby buried alive during the Korean War. I have heard the tragic cries of the neglected children looking for their mothers to feed them. When word got out that an epidemic had spread among the pigs and cows, I saw people bury live animals.

People are truly scary. A friend can become an enemy, and a husband can slice his wife into six pieces simply because they did not get along. Only people can deceive, conspire and betray. Therefore, people are the most fearful objects in the world.

And if somebody asked me "What is the most fearful thing besides people?" I would answer "money." You can only earn money by sweating and working like a slave for it. But that isn't the only reason why money is so scary. There probably aren't many people among the visually disabled who had visited so many churches, organizations, and individuals to ask for an offering of love. There probably aren't that many pastors who have gone around to so many churches to preach. Having done so, I have concluded that there's nothing scarier than money (next to people, of course). It is only understandable that money is thought of as a magic lantern in today's modern world. "Store your treasure in heaven." I try to engrave this teaching of Jesus in the depth of my heart.

The First Time I Saw Niagara Falls

The first time I visited America was in the 1970's. Before that time, I could only wonder what America was like. When I met American missionaries or soldiers, I thought America must be a country of abundance where everything was given to you with a mere snap of a finger. Such ideas were formed in my head because as a child I saw how the American soldiers freely gave candy, chocolate, and coca-cola to people. What kind of a country is America that it would give away food to people?

I was filled with expectations about what America was like. Imagining going to America even in my dreams, I pleaded with God to please let me just visit the place once. My childhood dreams and prayers finally came true. After going through a difficult process of entering America, the first place happened to visit was Chicago.

As I had expected, people wanted to buy me meals after I had spoken at a Korean-American Church. Some elders and elderesses gave me ten and twenty dollars for my personal use. When calculated, those tens and twenties added up to a considerable sum of money. Just like a beach is made up of millions of grains of sand and raindrops form a river, such money created a large amount of money. I sent over support offerings to the Mission Department and helped out struggling pastors with the money people gave me for my personal use.

While staying in such a bountiful country, I had an opportunity to visit Niagara Falls. There was a conference in New York. A group of pastors and I attended the morning session and decided to tour Niagara Falls during the afternoon. What did the picture of Niagara Falls look like which I had seen before I damaged my eyes? I tried to remember.

As soon as we arrived at the Falls, the sound of the cascading water and smell of the falls all seemed so mysterious. What is that sound? The powerful sound of the descending body of water seemed to me like an earthquake.

With the kind help of Reverend Kwon-Soon Chi, the group of pastors and I drifted onto the center of the lake in a boat. The dignified sound and tremendous waterfall seen from the boat made me realize once again the mystery of God's creation.

The only thing that pained my heart was the thought, 'how much greater would this mystery and beauty have been if only I could see it with my two eyes...' I couldn't have been more envious of my friends' exclamations of amazement as they beheld the waterfall with their own eyes.

The Name I Always Want to Call: Mother

Everyone has a name he or she wants to call. If a couple shares a deep love for each other, they want to say and hear the other's name anywhere and everywhere.

My daughter was dating a student from the same school. The young man sent a letter to my daughter when he left on a trip. My wife and I happened to come across the letter and we read it. However, only one thing was repeated throughout the letter: My daughter's name. Her name alone decorated the entire page of the letter. I thought about how much he loved her to fill a whole page with just her name. When two people are in love, they are prone to call their beloved's name even in their dreams.

The name of the single person I long to call out is "Mom." Although I have turned sixty already, I still want to call out the name Mom. Why is that? Because not only did I never receive my mother's love, but I was an orphan who didn't have the freedom to call anyone Mother. When I heard my friends call their own mother, I was envious to death.

When I was at my aunt's house, she once told me to peel a basket of beans on a fine autumn afternoon. I did as I was told for hours on end. After finishing my chore, I called out tenderly, "Aunt! I'm done!" My aunt replied, "I don't even want to hear your voice. You give me the chills. Don't even call me your aunt," and she threw the bean peels at me. I was so sad. I was afraid to call her 'aunt' from that point on. It worried me that I might get a beating for calling her 'aunt.' In moments like those, I half went crazy with thoughts of my mother.

Ah! The name I long to call with all my life, 'Mother.' When will I ever get to freely call that name over and over again?

My Request to
the Korean Churches

That Can't Be

In 1970, I toured Japan, America, and Canada. On Sundays, I spoke at different churches and during the weekdays, I went around with friends, visiting and observing schools and facilities for the visually disabled. Everywhere I went, the only thing I could think of was how everything seemed to be so conveniently designed for the visually disabled. It was heavenly indeed. Exquisite buildings, well structured educational programs, experienced faculty, and the way in which they treated the visually disabled with respect all appeared to be so beautiful and worthy of envy.

Their meals were high in nutrition, comparable to food consumed by millionaires in Korea. I thought about when Korean visually disabled citizens would receive such an education and training so that they too might become useful leaders in our society. Deep in such thoughts, I could not stop the flowing of tears. I encouraged myself with the faint ray of hope as I thought and prayed, 'If God is with us, such days will surely come.'

In nearby Japan and America, many social organizations and churches played a major role in donating handsome amounts to build a social welfare system for the visually disabled. But in our country, several pastors and elders not only rejected and interfered with such projects, but also took advantage of them by profiting off real estate transactions for their own gain. However, I give my full praise and appreciation to people who stood in the front lines giving donations and making the birth of the Siloam Eye Hospital possible.

Message to the Korean Churches

It has been 115 years since the gospel came into our country. In fact, Korea is one of the earliest underdeveloped country to come in contact with the gospel. There has been rapid development of churches and Christian organizations. Even through the bitter experience of the Korean War, Christianity and churches grew exponentially. Currently, Korea has as many megachurches as America, Canada, or Germany. This is, without doubt, something to be proud of.

However, it is plain to see that until now, the church has focused its ministry on non-disabled people; the church has not even given 1% of their attention to the disabled population. There aren't that many churches where they have set up accessible facilities for their disabled members. I think with regret that despite the 115 years of Christianity in Korea, there isn't a single sound church for the visually disabled today. The 200,000 blind, and over a million disabled people in Korea need to hear the gospel. Why is it that the spiritual leaders and members of the church neglect the ministry to the disabled?

Twelve years ago, we were able to establish a church for the visually disabled. However, we made one mistake. Although the church was built, the location did not allow safe travel. The roads leading to the church were extremely dangerous and loaded with various obstacles. When I met visually disabled members serving and praising at church faithfully, I felt pride welling up from within.

Churches for healthy non-disabled people are often built in safe places without much traffic. Then why is it that a church for people who cannot see must be planted on high hills where there is much danger of getting hurt? We should give some serious thought to such a sad reality of our country.

One of the earliest records of Jesus' ministry shows us how he cared compassionately for the poor, weak and disabled. He took great interest in them and gave them hope, joy and happiness. It wouldn't be an exaggeration to say that the gospel of Jesus Christ is really for the weak, sick and disabled.

Is it because today's spiritual leaders and members, who believe and serve that very Jesus, lack calling and love for the disabled that they can care less whether a church for the visually disabled is built on a steep hill or not?

Each church insists on having a retreat center, prayer garden and gym of their own for their members. Shouldn't there be a model church to spread love and gospel to the disabled who are in discomfort and pain?

A church cannot say they have fulfilled their duty to the disabled by buying them a few sacks of rice, a couple sets of warm winter clothes, or several boxes of noodles during Christmas time. It is my request that the Korean churches will get involved in the social reformations of the 21st century to improve the conditions of disabled citizens with fitting sophistication and a solemn sense of calling.

The Disabled Are
Also Children of God

Until now, the word 'disabled' evoked distasteful feelings of pity or charity. For that reason, there were many instances of families locking up their disabled members in the house, providing them with the bare minimum of food. They did nothing to help them but secretly, or sometimes openly, waited for their death. Such abuses stem from a misunderstanding and mistaken perception of disabled people not only in society but in the churches as well.

When I had graduated from college and seminary, I applied to take the ordination exam. Renowned pastors, recognized for their intelligence and sophistication, failed me on my ordination exam based on the reasoning that a pastor must be perfect, without blemish or disability. However, we see many instances of disabled people throughout history who have changed and impacted the world and church.

Milton, the author of *Paradise Lost,* had a visual disability; the king of the composers, Beethoven, had a hearing disability; King Alexander, who conquered the world, was a hunchback; The authoritarian Napoleon who conquered Europe had no use of his legs. John Bunyun wrote his well-known *Pilgrim's Progress* as a disabled man in prison; President Franklin Roosevelt ruled America in his wheelchair; Fanny Jane Crosby, a visually disabled musician, decorates page after page of the hymnal. And the Apostle Paul who had very weak eyes and suffered from epilepsy gave his all in spreading the message of Christ in the midst of his pain.

Many physically disabled people have been used to enlighten the dark world, give hope to the hopeless, and inspire those in despair. As we read the above accounts of disabled people, we must examine ourselves. How much do we love them and give them the respect they deserve?

Countless churches in Japan and America set aside 30 to 40 percent of their yearly budget to help those who are living in the dark shadows or their community. What about Korean churches? They are satisfied with giving a few boxes of noodles, a couple of sacks of rice or a few thousand won during Christmas. Disabled people are only looked upon as objects of pity and disgust.

During every disabled recognition month, there is one thing I would like to emphasize to the Korean churches and communities. Korean churches must create a definite strategy to help the disabled who are as much heavenly citizens as any believer and must help them with offerings of love. In another words, the Korean churches need a higher understanding of disabled people, and the realization that the disabled are also part of their community.

Becoming a Guardian Angel
For Our Neighbors

On June 1, 1998, I was chosen as one of five people to receive the Ho-ahm Social Service Award. Giving all the glory to God, I sincerely prayed that someday, I may join hands with all people in spreading the love of Christ.

I overcame many hurdles and obstacles since I lost my eyesight in 1950 with people around me to help. I do not know when it began but I found myself playing the role of guardian angel to my neighbors. This role is one that truly pleases God. I will run any place I am needed to sow hope and light for the visually disabled.

The help and assistance of many people has brought me thus far. I can never forget the kind care of those who had helped me with their everlasting love. I also thank all those who came a long way to help me and encourage me.

I try to live every moment of my life with a positive attitude, sharing everything I have with others. I plan to fight a good fight and run the race marked out for me like the Apostle Paul. I will try my best to live the rest of my life sharing the love of Christ and His comfort with anyone who comes to me for help. I ask for your prayers that such thoughts of mine will bear good fruit in Christ Jesus our Lord.

Now is the Time to Utilize
the Power of Love

Through the discovery of fire, humanity advanced to the point of forming a scientifically developed and cultured world. But beginning in modern times, the human discovery of fossil fuels marked the beginning of the end of the world. How could we have predicted the wild climate changes introduced through global warming?

People's failure to find another energy source which could counteract fossil fuels slowly led to the destruction of the world. Apocalyptic writings, movies, and predictions have become the utmost interest of the human population. The 20th century boils over with all sorts of apocalyptic ideas and trends.

However, with the impending destruction of the world hanging over our shoulders, the world is busier than ever trying to invent new technology to make our lives more perfect and enjoyable. It makes me wonder if world evangelism can indeed provide the new energy humanity can live on.

From where should we look for the energy that will prevent the destruction of the human race? Is there an energy that has never been used by the humanity? With all the new age movements, it seems as though people are reverting back to the Oriental practice of yoga and other relaxation exercises in their attempt to translate their natural energy to a supernatural one.

But even that energy runs short on supply. People try to use meditation to reach a heightened state of spiritual existence or even a state of nirvana by suppressing their desires and wishes—but that too seems to lose its potential in the face of harsh reality.

Today, many initiators of peace movements try to create major changes within the field of politics, economy, agriculture, and medicine. I believe some of them might even be Christians. Scholars of plant breeding who are trying to bring about an agricultural revolution and peace advocates try to use such energy for the good of the mankind.

A war analyst once did research on the causes of war. He found that wars take place not only during times of wealth and abundance but also when natural disasters and famine dominate the lives of the people. Wars also happened with the birth of cultural revolutions. Because of this, I believe peace movements are limited in that they are influenced by pressures.

Through my short life, I have come to realize one energy people dread to use. If only we can perfectly produce this energy and put it to use, then mankind can immediately be saved from any pit of depression or despair.

What is the energy of love? Love's energy has the power to elevate a person's existence; it has the spiritual mystery of acknowledging man's dignity.

We usually understand and limit the power of love to love between parents and children, husband and wife, brothers and sisters, lovers, love for one's country, or neighborly love. We understand such love between our kin. But how can humanity utilize this mysterious strength of love to promote the peace and welfare of mankind?

I am assured that the mission work for the visually disabled and ministry of restoring sight utilize the power of love. Evangelism to the visually disabled which does not act as a conduit of love is a ministry that only exists in theory.

If my sacrifice and dedication are merely justifications of my righteousness, I am only negating the power of love. Without having correct perception and strategy to use such a power of love in a positive way, we will never be able to create the foundation of a ministry for the visually disabled.

There is a reason we view restoration of sight as a means of rebirth. Blindness represents temporary death and restoration of sight through an operation symbolizes a resurrection. The mysterious power of love comes back alive with the eye operation because such love was poured into the very process of that ministry. Love's energy has the power to continuously regenerate the miracle of love. I always witness such moving scenes in the ministry for the blind.

It is truly a miracle that a person who had lost his sight could see again through an eye operation. I am confident that the power of love has the supernatural strength to make miracles happen. I now realize that the mysterious power God planted in man at the time of creation is this energy of love. That is the conclusion I reached as I ministered to the visually disabled for the last fifty years of my life, since losing my eyesight. If someone asks me what my confession of faith is, I would say, "It is to find God's hidden power of love in man and to activate that mysterious strength."

My past life has been a continuation of one unspeakable suffering after another. It was a bloody path and a desert land of hard work, but, in my heart, God's cosmos was perpetually being uncovered which led me to experience amazing comfort. All this was possible because I had discovered the mysterious power of love.

To me, salvation is the application of God's love activated within the given relationship of Christ. The faith that can enter into the reality of the invisible world through the power of love is the faith that saves. The hope of the world lies in the application of the power of love within the psychological and spiritual realm. It is my prayer that everyone can experience the power of love I have experienced in my ministry for the visually disabled by humbly serving one another.

To the Readers

Once I Was Poor and Lonely But Now I am Rich

I lived a poor and miserable life. I still remember staying by myself in an uninsulated dorm room whenever winter break rolled around. It was also during those days I had to stretch a single serving of ramen instant noodles to last me for three meals.

One cold snowy winter day, I went outside in search of food to buy with a few coins I had managed to save. I lost my sense of direction and ended up falling into a snow pit, losing one of my shoes. Digging through the snow with frozen hands to recover my shoe, feels like only yesterday. Just the mere mention of those days makes me shiver. It made me envious to imagine how at that very moment, many of my friends were enjoying love and home-cooked meals in the safety and warmth of their home.

During vacations, deciding where to stay always posed as a big problem. On top of that, I didn't have much money. Eating three meals a day was always almost impossible. I often thought to myself, 'When will I ever escape from this chain of poverty and loneliness?' To be free from them was my biggest dream and hope. My youthful school years drifted away, oppressed by poverty and loneliness. I often use the expression, "heaven is my blanket and the earth is my bed." No one can fathom how pathetic my existence was. I eagerly waited for the day when I would be wealthy with a huge family.

But now, all my dreams have come true beyond measure. I have became wealthy. By 'wealth', I do not mean I own a big house and many material possessions. We live in a small apartment but I am fully satisfied. It is because I have a big, loving family: My wife Jung-Ja, my oldest daughter Eun-Hae, my second daughter, Ji- Hae, adopted daughter Eun-Mi, son-in-law Byung-Tak, granddaughter Elizabeth, the 80 employees at the Siloam Eye Hospital, and 90 more workers at the rehabilitation center. Of course, I have countless co-workers and friends scattered all over the world. They, too, are all part of my earthly family.

Having so many trusted co-workers and friends naturally gave me many homes to stay at wherever I go. In Toronto Canada, there are the members of the Toronto Association for the Visually Disabled; In Washington, there is a Siloam Funding Organization, and in Chicago, there are many co-workers and friends of the Midwest Siloam Funding Organization. They provide me with lodgings, food and funds for our Siloam Eye

Hospital. I am blessed with so many families and homes. How can I not be happy?

I have people who will welcome me into their house in every part of the world. I, who lived in utter poverty, now live in unspeakable wealth. Furthermore, what kind of hospital restores the sight of thousands of people per year free of charge? I take great pride when I realize the Siloam Eye Hospital is unique in this way. But it doesn't mean that Siloam has funds flowing out of its pockets. We simply make the best out of the little we are given for each day, and it adds up to giving sight to thousands of people every year. All this is a result of my family, friends, and co-workers contributing their unconditional love. Although I was truly poor, I am happy and grateful that I can now live an abundant life with my family. I would like to live the rest of my life, serving and sharing everything with the poor. Such thoughts are the source of my true wealth.

The Sun-Tae Kim
I Know

Last Words by Friends

The One Who Has Presented Light in the Name of Christ

Rev. Uye-Woong Yoo

(Moderator for the Presbyterian Church of Korea,

Senior Pastor of Dorim Church)

Mark Chapter 2 contains the beautiful story of four friends who carry their paralytic friend to Jesus. The friends have brought their paralyzed friend at all cost to Jesus. Jesus saw their faith and said to the paralyzed man, "Your sins have been forgiven." What a moving scene.

Reverend Sun-Tae Kim is a great pastor whom the entire world is proud of. I think Reverend Kim is like those friends in Mark chapter 2 in many ways. He has introduced Jesus to numerous visually disabled people who were living in confinement and darkness. Not only did he grant them spiritual eyes to see the eternal light of Jesus, he also opened their physical eyes through the work of the Siloam Eye Hospital. Reverend Kim has brought the light to many people in the name of Christ.

He is a precious individual who has overcome his own disability and devoted his entire life to looking after others with the same disability. He always puts them before himself. We too should be like the four friends in the gospel of Mark by helping Reverend Kim lead more people from darkness into light. I congratulate him for publishing his autobiography. I am confident that many people will experience the wonderful grace of God through this book.

The One Who Lost This World but Gained Heaven

Rev. Won-Suk Han

(Moderator of the Presbyterian Church of Korea)

Although we cannot trace back the origin of the visually disabled in our society, we know they have existed at least since the Old Testament times. The New Testament especially abounds with stories of the blind. And all the visually disabled are portrayed as being poor and destitute. Such portrayals of the blind in the olden times are only too understandable. What could they have done in those days? They had to survive by begging and receiving help from others. There are people with many kinds of disabilities but I feel for the visually disabled people the most. What would it be like if one was to live with a blindfold over his eyes for an entire day? And how great would the pain be for the family who has a visually disabled member?

I came to know Reverend Kim while he was studying at the Presbyterian Seminary. It completely amazed me that a visually disabled person was studying at a regular university as a graduate student.

Humor Even in Midst of Hardship

I have been told that he could regain even a little bit of his sight if he receives an eye operation. But he refuses to be operated on because he says that he cannot neglect the many other visually disabled for his own sake. He has decided to devote his entire life to them and them alone.

He has played the piano and flute whenever he needed to ease himself of the pain and the hurt. He plays by memorizing the music scores. And professionals have judged his musical skills to be quite outstanding. Whenever he is introduced to someone, he remembers their name for many years to come. He also makes others laugh.

It was about ten years ago when I met up with Reverend Kim in America and back to Korea on the same plane. I guided him and made sure he arrived well. We arrived at Kimpo Airport and after all the procedural checks, I made sure he met up with his family who was waiting for him at the airport.

But according to a rumor I heard later on, he had supposedly said that he had a difficult time guiding the moderator from America to Korea. I wonder how the listeners must have responded to a visually disabled person guiding a seeing person from America to Korea. In such ways, he makes others laugh.

Not only that, he often says to ladies he meets for the first time, "You are very pretty." Having received such a compliment from a blind person, she thinks, 'How does a person who cannot see know what I look like?' And throws the question, "Can you see just a little?" Then he usually responds, "I can see everything that I can see," and smiles.

Reverend Kim is also a man of loyalty. I always tell Reverend Kim that a person must be a man of loyalty and only those who are loyal are true human beings. He never betrays a person he has put his trust in. He believes that one should not even fellowship with those who lack loyalty.

Reverend Kim has already accomplished seemingly impossible tasks. But I believe finishing up what he has started will be a much greater task.

With cooperation of the American eye doctors, Reverend Kim has restored sight to many outcasts throughout Korea. Furthermore, he and his missions team have visited Beijing to perform free operations to over 400 Korean-Chinese; In the Philippines, he also restored sight of forty natives in Bagio area. His Siloam Mobile Eye Hospital, a converted 46-passenger bus is sent on weekly missions trips all around the nation, spreading the gospel and giving sight to the blind. I do not doubt that he has greater plans he is thinking of carrying out in the future.

If America boasts of Helen Keller and Japan boasts of its visually disabled philosopher, Iwabashi Takeoh, Korea can boast of her hero, Sun Tae Kim, who is the president of an eye hospital, an evangelist to the blind, a reverend, and a doctor.

Lastly, I cannot leave out his wife who has supported him all the way. As a mother of two, an elderess at her church, and as a wife of a pastor, I pray that God's blessings will abound throughout her life. May God bless Reverend Kim with His everlasting blessings.

A Single Stem of Flower

Rev. Jae-Hong Han

Pastor of the New Light Church in New York

I encountered a mysterious flower that brightens the entire world. In the presence of that flower, even the most proud person becomes self conscious. I always think about how great it would be if the whole world was covered with such flowers.

"Where can one find such a flower? What is the name of that flower?" You might ask.

"Close your eyes and listen to the rest of my story. You will no doubt leave with the name in your heart by the time I'm done." I would comfort my listener.

This flower is a fragrance to the blind, and a sound of hope more intimate than your spouse. It is the energy that restores your values to live a life of worth, and a rare puff of breath that rekindles the dying flame. I met this flower at Trenton, the capital of New Jersey. Back then, I was busy finishing up my seminary studies while doing my ministry. The flower that appeared before me at that time contained within him every kind of tragedy. But it was strange that I was able to smell fragrance completely devoid of any sense of despair. I found energy from his laughter. I felt warmth in his words. From then on, our friendship blossomed to no end.

I have never met such a flower before, nor have I ever heard of him. Our meeting merely lasted a couple of hours. And I was no longer able to see that flower for several months. Although it seemed as though I forgot about him on the outside, I couldn't deny that the flower had taken deep root within my heart.

Four years later, I was doing ministry in San Francisco. I received a phone call in the deep of the night. The caller was that very flower. I remembered our meeting from several years back. I longed to smell his fragrance again.

The next day, we had a joyous reunion. That flower had the power to retain names of the people he had met even only once. He asked me if my son was doing well. Calling my son by name. The flower must have exuded his fragrance to a countless number of people. Yet, he remembered the name of every one of them.

I firmly grasped his hand. I was moved to participate in the work of that flower. So I met with several pastors. I explained to them all about his ministry until my mouth went dry. Several people's hearts agreed to hold a joint conference. Of course, the speaker was that flower. We listened to his testimony with tears in our eyes. Four days of blessed conference finally came to end and yielded much good fruit. One housewife donated twenty 100 dollar bills which she had saved up since the time she got married. I was touched. Back then, a person could receive an eye operation with just $200.

According to the Korean national statistics, there are hundreds of thousands of partially blind and 200,000 blind people in Korea. Out of those 200,000, almost 100,000 can regain their sight with an eye operation. It is tragic that they cannot see because they do not have $200.

A few years later, I found myself in New York City. I started my ministry with a strong conviction from the Lord. The flower kept in touch with me. We soon met again with joyous hearts. I invited him to stay at my place for several days. It was a good opportunity for me to admire and smell his fragrance. Flowers usually grow more beautiful with each look, and the fragrance sweetens with each smell. He was no exception. I saw and heard the integrity in his words, laughter and manners. I felt ashamed of myself in his presence.

Although that flower could not see the sun, he possessed the sun in his heart. We experienced God's mighty work through him and confirmed the truth that nothing is impossible through God. I also learned that I wasn't in charge of doing God's work, but God used whoever He pleased according to His plans.

Most people have a tendency to kiss up to the stronger and trample on the weak. But as always, he looked after those who were weaker than himself with such tender love and care. He was in the habit of serving others rather than being served. He taught us so much by giving everything to others when he himself had every reason to receive from them. Someone had once said that it is better for a person to be worn out than to rust. How great it would be to live in such a way.

Whenever I see that flower, I am reminded of refined silver. He could see the faces of his beloved family if he goes through an eye operation. But he refuses for two reasons.

The first reason is money. His operation costs would well equal the operation costs of at least several hundred mildly visually disabled people. Even though he can't see, he is more satisfied when others can see because of him. Such selflessness should be praised in this age of selfishness. I asked myself if I would be able to forego my own sight for the sake of hundreds of others. An affirmative answer did not come easy. Sometimes, I think that God gave him such a disability so that he might not stray from the path he is treading on now. I am always proud that he is my good friend and older brother in Christ.

The other reason he refuses the operation is because he is afraid that once his eyesight is restored, people will not be as cooperative as before. If he loses support, where would he get the funds to look after his visually disabled brothers and sisters? He considers being a good neighbor to his suffering friends more important than restoring his own sight. Perhaps his fragrance never fades because he lives for others.

Siloam Eye Hospital, located in Kang-Suh-Ku, Seoul

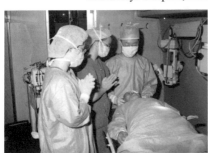

The Siloam Eye Hospital was established on February 17, 1986 to commemorate the 100th anniversary since the introduction of Christianity to Korea.

Our modern 4-storey hospital complex along with its annex, is fully-equipped with the latest medical equipment and is capable of providing the highest standard of medical care.

It is our mission to reach out to the 200,000 blind and 5 million visually impaired living throughout Korea--and also to our less fortunate brothers and sisters suffering in the Third-World countries.

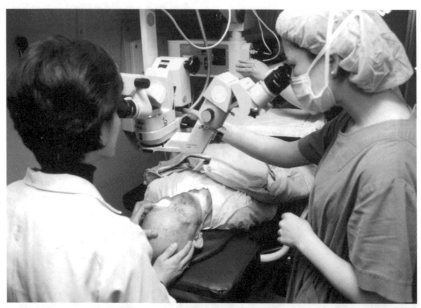

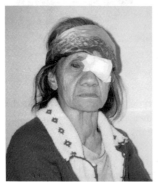

Since the launching of our mobile eye hospital project in March of 1995, Siloam has been reaching out to the remote islands and farming areas to provide service for those without appropriate medical care. The dedicated Siloam Mobile team has been making 50 trips every year.

The Mobile Eye Hospital is a converted 46-passenger bus donated by the Samsung Corporation. It is staffed by a total of 10 ophthalmologists, optometrists, nurses and administrative personnel and is fully equipped to diagnose and treat patients, and even to perform major operations.

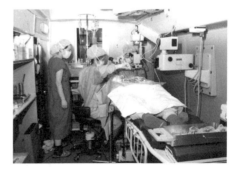

The mobile team is sent out on weekly mission trips--to leper colonies, orphanages, youth correctional facilities, prisons, homes for the elderly, poor neighborhoods and schools for the blind throughout Korea.

Angel's Voice Choir

With the Choir, after finishing a revival tour of the US.

Reverend Kyung-Jik Han 's particular interest for the visually disabled strengthened our ministry for the blind.

A photograph from my high school days

Our wedding portrait

With my wife at graduation from the
Presbyterian Seminary in Korea

Our first daughter
Eun-Hae's wedding

With my wife Jung-Ja and two daughters,
Eun-Hae and Ji-Hae.

Ji-Hae's wedding

Elizabeth, our granddaugher

Eun-Mi, my adopted daughter

272

Receiving the Presidential Medal of Honor in 1985[left] and the Soongsil Human Achievement Award[below].

[left] Soongsil University awarded its alumni with an Honorary Doctorate of Philosophy in October, 2000.

[right] Receiving a Doctorate of Ministry from McCormick Theological Seminary(Chicago), June 1993.

[left] At the recognition ceremony on June '98 hosted by Ho-Ahm Foundation of Korea. The foundation presented me with the Social Services Award for my work in restoring sight.

People who look for the light

Contact Information for
Siloam Eye Hospital

Siloam Eye Hospital
512-5 Deung-chon 2 Dong
Kang-seo ku, Seoul, Korea

Tel: 82-2-653-5561, 82-2-650-0700

http://www.siloam.co.kr